T0254832

Lecture Notes in Artificial Intelligence 13403

Subseries of Lecture Notes in Computer Science

More information about this subseries at https://link.springer.com/bookseries/1244

Tanya Braun · Diana Cristea ·
Robert Jäschke (Eds.)

Graph-Based Representation and Reasoning

27th International Conference
on Conceptual Structures, ICCS 2022
Münster, Germany, September 12–15, 2022
Proceedings

 Springer

Editors
Tanya Braun 🆔
University of Münster
Münster, Germany

Diana Cristea 🆔
Babes-Bolyai University
Cluj-Napoca, Romania

Robert Jäschke 🆔
Humboldt-Universität zu Berlin
Berlin, Germany

ISSN 0302-9743   ISSN 1611-3349 (electronic)
Lecture Notes in Artificial Intelligence
ISBN 978-3-031-16662-4   ISBN 978-3-031-16663-1 (eBook)
https://doi.org/10.1007/978-3-031-16663-1

LNCS Sublibrary: SL7 – Artificial Intelligence

This Springer imprint is published by the registered company Springer Nature Switzerland AG
The registered company address is: Gewerbestrasse 11, 6330 Cham, Switzerland

Preface

The 27th edition of the International Conference on Conceptual Structures (ICCS 2022) took place in Münster, Germany, during 12–15 September, 2022, under the title "Graph-based Representation and Reasoning". Since 1993, ICCS has been a yearly venue for publishing and discussing new research methods along with their practical applications in the context of graph-based representation formalisms and reasoning, with a broad interpretation of its namesake conceptual structures. Topics of this year's conference include modeling and knowledge representation, lattices and formal concept analyses, and decision support and prediction. The call asked for regular papers reporting on novel technical contributions and 13 submissions were received. The committee decided to accept 8 papers which corresponds to an acceptance rate of 61%. Each submission received two to four reviews, with 3.5 reviews on average. In total, our Program Committee members, supported by two additional reviewers, delivered 45 reviews. The review process was double-blind, with papers anonymized for the reviewers and reviewer names unknown to the authors. We organized a bidding on papers to ensure that reviewers received papers within their field of expertise. The response to the bidding process allowed us to assign each paper to reviewers who had expressed an interest in reviewing a particular paper. The final decision was made after the authors had a chance to reply to the initial reviews via a rebuttal to correct factual errors or answer reviewer questions. We believe this procedure ensured that only high-quality contributions were presented at the conference.

Next to the regular contributions, we were delighted to host two tutorials, "Data & AI Ethics" by Jesse Dinneen (Humboldt-Universität zu Berlin, Germany) as well as "Forgetting in Knowledge Representation and Reasoning" by Kai Sauerwald (FernUniversität in Hagen, Germany). Furthermore, we were honoured to receive three keynotes talks: "Tractable Probabilistic Models for Ethical and Causal AI" by Vaishak Belle (University of Edinburgh, UK), "Qualitative Spatial Evaluation of Sketch Maps" by Angela Schwering (University of Münster, Germany), and "Neuroconceptual Processing for Learning, Reasoning, and Language Understanding" by Arun Majumdar and John F. Sowa (both ARD Global, LLC). Note that this volume provides the extended abstracts of the keynote talks "Tractable Probabilistic Models for Ethical and Causal AI" by Vaishak Belle and "Neurosymbolic Computation with the Logic Virtual Machine" by Arun Majumdar and John F. Sowa.

As general chair and program chairs, we would like to thank our speakers for their inspiring and insightful talks. We would like to thank the Program Committee members and additional reviewers for their work. Without their substantial voluntary contribution, it would not have been possible to set up such a high-quality conference program. We would also like thank EasyChair for their support in handling submissions and Springer for their support in making these proceedings possible. Our institutions, the University of Münster, Germany, Babeş-Bolyai University of Cluj-Napoca, Romania, and Humboldt-Universität zu Berlin, Germany also provided support for our participation, for which we

are grateful. Last but not least, we thank the ICCS steering committee for their ongoing
support and dedication to ICCS.

June 2022

Tanya Braun
Diana Cristea
Robert Jäschke

Organization

General Chair

Tanya Braun   University of Münster, Germany

Program Committee Chairs

Diana Cristea   Babeş-Bolyai University of Cluj-Napoca, Romania

Robert Jäschke   Humboldt-Universität zu Berlin, Germany

Steering Committee

Tanya Braun   University of Münster, Germany
Madalina Croitoru   LIRMM, Université Montpellier, France
Dominik Endres   University of Marburg, Germany
Simon Polovina   Sheffield Hallam University, UK
Uta Priss   Ostfalia University of Applied Sciences, Germany
Sebastian Rudolph   Technische Universität Dresden, Germany

Program Committee

Simon Andrews   Sheffield Hallam University, UK
Moulin Bernard   Laval University, Canada
Peggy Cellier   IRISA, INSA Rennes, France
Licong Cui   University of Texas Health Science Center at Houston, USA
Harry Delugach   University of Alabama in Huntsville, USA
Florent Domenach   Akita International University, Japan
Dominik Endres   University of Marburg, Germany
Jérôme Euzenat   Inria and Université Grenoble Alpes, France
Marcel Gehrke   University of Lübeck, Germany
Raji Ghawi   Technical University of Munich, Germany
Ollivier Haemmerlé   IRIT, University of Toulouse, France
Tom Hanika   University of Kassel, Germany
Nathalie Hernandez   IRIT, University of Toulouse, France
Dmitry Ignatov   National Research University Higher School of Economics, Russia
Adil Kabbaj   INSEA, Morocco

Hamamache Kheddouci	Université Claude Bernard Lyon 1, France
Léonard Kwuida	Bern University of Applied Sciences, Switzerland
Jérôme Lang	CNRS, LAMSADE, Université Paris Dauphine-PSL, France
Natalia Loukachevitch	Moscow State University, Russia
Philippe Martin	LIM, Université de la Réunion, France
Amedeo Napoli	Loria Nancy, France
Sergei Obiedkov	National Research University Higher School of Economics, Russia
Nathalie Pernelle	LIPN, Université Sorbonne Paris Nord, France
Simon Polovina	Sheffield Hallam University, UK
Gerd Stumme	University of Kassel, Germany
Christian Săcărea	Babeş-Bolyai University, Romania
Guoqiang Zhang	University of Texas Health Science Center at Houston, USA
Diana Şotropa	Babeş-Bolyai University of Cluj-Napoca, Romania

Additional Reviewers

Hirth, Johannes
Lalou, Mohammed
Li, Xiaojin

Neurosymbolic Computation with the Logic Virtual Machine (Abstract of Invited Talk)

Arun K. Majumdar and John F. Sowa

ARD Global, LLC

`galaxiesmerge1@verizon.net`, `jfsowa@alum.mit.edu`

The Logic Virtual Machine (LVM) supports ISO Standard Prolog with tensors as a native datatype. The tensors can represent graphs or networks of any kind. For most applications, the great majority of elements of the tensors are zero, and the nonzero elements are bit strings of arbitrary length. Those bit strings may encode symbolic information, or they may represent integers of any size.

If the nodes encode symbolic information, the tensors may represent conceptual graphs, knowledge graphs, or the logics of the Semantic Web, Formal UML, and other knowledge representation languages. As an extension of Prolog, LVM can perform logical reasoning or other kinds of transformations on or with those notations.

Since the bit strings in the tensors may be interpreted as integers of arbitrary length, operations on those tensors may perform the same kinds of subsymbolic computations used in neural networks. As an extension of Prolog, LVM can relate neural tensors and symbolic tensors for neurosymbolic reasoning.

Since the symbolic and subsymbolic tensors are supported by the same LVM system, operations that relate them can be performed with a single Prolog statement. For special-purpose operations and connections to other systems, LVM can invoke subroutines in Python or C.

By combining the strengths of symbolic AI with neural networks, LVM spans the full range learning and reasoning methods developed for either or both. Three major applications are computational chemistry, sentiment analysis of natural language documents, and fraud analysis in financial transactions.

All three applications take advantage of the unique LVM features: precise symbolic reasoning, neural-network style of learning, and the ability to analyze huge volumes of graphs by precise methods or probabilistic methods. Applications in computational chemistry have obtained excellent results in molecular toxicology for the EPA TOX21 challenge. Applications in sentiment analysis combine Prolog's advantages for natural language processing (NLP) with a neural-network style of learning. Applications in financial fraud analysis combine NLP methods with learning and reasoning methods that must be accurate to fractions of a cent.

Contents

Invited Talk

Tractable Probabilistic Models
for Ethical AI

Vaishak Belle[✉]

University of Edinburgh & Alan Turing Institute, London, UK
vbelle@ed.ac.uk

Abstract. Among the many ethical dimensions that arise in the use of ML technology, three stand out as immediate and profound: enabling the interpretability of the underlying decision boundary, addressing the potential for learned algorithms to become biased against certain groups, and capturing blame and responsibility for a system's outcomes. In this talk, we advocate for a research program that seeks to bridge tractable (probabilistic) models for knowledge acquisition with rich models of autonomous agency that draw on philosophical notions of beliefs, intentions, causes and effects.

1 Motivation

Machine learning (ML) techniques have become pervasive across a range of different applications, and are now widely used in areas as disparate as recidivism prediction, consumer credit-risk analysis, and insurance pricing [8,25]. Likewise, in the physical world, machine learning models are critical components in autonomous agents such as robotic surgeons and self-driving cars. Among the many societal/ethical dimensions that arise in the use of ML technology in such applications, three stand out as immediate and profound. First, to increase trust and accommodate human insight, interpretability of the underlying decision boundary is essential. Second, there is the potential for learned algorithms to become biased against certain groups, which needs to be addressed. Third, in so much that the decisions of ML models impact society, both virtually (e.g., denying a loan) and physically (e.g., accidentally driving into a pedestrian), the enabling of blame and responsibility is a significant challenge.

Many definitions have been proposed in the literature for such ethical considerations [2,19], but there is considerable debate about whether a formal notion is appropriate at all, given the rich social contexts that occur in human-machine interactions. Valid arguments are also made about the challenges of model building and deployment [10,11]: everything from data collection to ascribing responsibility when technology goes awry can demonstrate and amplify abuse of power

This article is a written version of the keynote to be given at *27th International Conference on Conceptual Structures*, September 2022, Münster, Germany. A preliminary version of this work was also presented at the *Critical Perspectives on Artificial Intelligence Ethics Conference* in Edinburgh, UK, 2020. The author was supported by a Royal Society University Research Fellowship.

T. Braun et al. (Eds.): ICCS 2022, LNCS 13403, pp. 3–8, 2022.
https://doi.org/10.1007/978-3-031-16663-1_1

and privilege. Such issues are deeply intertwined with legal and regulatory problems [15,32].

Be that as it may, what steps can be taken to enable ethical decision-making a reality in AI systems? Human-in-the-loop systems are arguably required given the aforementioned debate [24,34], but such loops still need to interface with an automated system of considerable sophistication that in the very least reasons about the possible set of actions. In particular, simply delegating responsibility of critical decisions to humans in an ad hoc fashion can be problematic. Often critical actions can be hard to identify immediately and it is only the ramification of those actions that raise alarm, in which case it might be too late for the human to fix. Moreover, understanding the model's rationale is a challenge in itself, as represented by the burgeoning field of explainable artificial intelligence [4,14,29]. So a careful delineation is needed as to which parts are automated, which parts are delegated to humans, which parts can be obtained from humans a-priori (i.e., so-called *knowledge-enhanced machine learning* [9]), but also how systems can be made to reason about their environment so that they are able to capture and deliberate on their choices, however limiting their awareness of the world might be. In the very least, the latter capacity offers an additional layer of protection, control and explanation before delegating, as the systems can point out which beliefs and observations led to their actions.

2   Two-Pronged Approach

In that regard, our view is that a two-pronged approach is needed in the least. On the one hand, we have to draw on philosophical notions and look to formalise them, as attempted by the knowledge representation community. Indeed this community has looked to capture beliefs, desires, intentions, and causality in service of formal notions that provide an idealised perspective on epistemology grounded in, say, a putative robot's mental state [5,16,21,22]. But the topic of knowledge acquisition, i.e., how the relevant propositions can be acquired from data is largely left open. Moreover, the topic of reasoning, i.e., of computing truths of acquired knowledge is a long-standing challenge owing to the intractability of propositional reasoning and the undecidability of first-order logic, and many higher-order logics.

On the other hand, although machine learning systems do successfully address acquisition from data, mainstream methods focus on atomic classification tasks, and not the kind of complex reasoning over physical and mental deliberation that humans are adept in. (There are exceptions from robotics and reinforcement learning, of course, but these all attempt some form of mental state modeling [1], and in the very least, reasoning about possible worlds [31].) Moreover, issues about robustness in the presence of approximate computations remain.

In this talk, we advocate for a research program that seeks to apply tractable (probabilistic) models to problems in fair machine learning and automated reasoning of moral principles. Such models are compilation targets for propositional and finite-domain relational logic, and so can represent certain types of knowledge representation languages. They can also be learned from data. We report on a few preliminary results [7,12,17,23,26–28,33,35]. Firstly, we discuss results on studying causality-related properties in such models, and extracting counterfactual explanations from them. On the topic of fairness, it is shown that the approach enables an effective technique for determining the statistical relationships between protected attributes and other training variables. This could then be applied as a pre-processing step for computing fair models. On the topic of moral responsibility, it is shown how models of moral scenarios and blameworthiness can be extracted and learnt automatically from data as well as how judgements be computed effectively. In both themes, the learning of the model can be conditioned on expert knowledge allowing us to represent and reason about the domain of interest in a principled fashion.

3 Closing Remarks

We conclude with key observations about the interplay between tractability, learning and knowledge representation in the context of ethical decision-making. Among other things, we observe that the tractable model paradigm is in its early years, at least as far capturing a broad range of knowledge representation languages is concerned, and moreover, there is altogether less emphasis on mental modeling and agency. (First-order expressiveness is yet another dimension for allowing richness in specifications, as are proposals with an explicit causal theory such as [30]). In contrast, readers may want to consult discussions in [23,24] on knowledge representation approaches where a more comprehensive model of the environment and its actors is considered, but where knowledge acquisition and learning are used in careful, limited ways.

Analogously, we observe that although many expressive languages [6,18] are known to compile to tractable models, this is purely from the viewpoint of reasoning, or more precisely, probabilistic query computation. What is likely needed is a set of strategies for reversing this pipeline: from a learned tractable model, we need to be able to infer high-level representations. In the absence of general strategies of that sort, the more modest proposal is perhaps to interleave declarative knowledge for high-level patterns but allow low-level patterns to be learnt, which then are altogether compiled for tractable inference.

Overall, the discussed results can be seen occupying positions on a spectrum: the fairness result simply provides a way to accomplish de-biasing, but does not engage with a specification of the users or the environment in any concrete way. Thus, it is closer to mainstream fairness literature. The moral reasoning result is richer in that sense, as it explicitly accounts for actors and their actions in the environment. However, it does not explicitly infer how these actions and effects might have come about – these might be acquired via learning, for example – nor does it reason about what role these actions play amongst multiple actors in the environment. Thus, clearly, in the long run, richer formal systems are needed, which might account for sequential actions [3] and multiple agents [20].

However, this reverts the position back to the issues of tractability and knowledge acquisition not being addressed in such proposals. So, the question is this: can we find ways to appeal to tractable probabilistic models (or other structures with analogous properties) with such rich formal systems? As mentioned, it is known that certain probabilistic logical theories can be reduced to such structures, so perhaps gentle extensions to those theories might suggest ways to integrate causal epistemic models and tractable learning.

Beyond that technical front, much work remains to be done, of course, in terms of delineating automated decision-making from delegation and notions of accountability [13]. It is also worth remaking that computational solutions of the sort discussed in the previous section do make strong assumptions about the environment in which the learning and acting happens. In a general setting, even data collection can amplify positions of privilege, and moreover, there are multiple opportunities for failure and misspecification [10,11]. Orchestrating a framework where this kind of information and knowledge can be communicated back to the automated system is not at all obvious, and is an open challenge. In that regard, the two-pronged approach is not advocated as a solution to such broader problems, and indeed, it is unclear whether abstract models can imbibe cultural and sociopolitical contexts in a straightforward manner. However, it at least allows us to specify norms for human-machine interaction, provide goals and situations to achieve, model the machine's beliefs, and allow the machine to entertain models of the user's knowledge. Ultimately, the hope is that the expressiveness argued for offers additional protection, control and explanation during the deployment of complex systems with machine learning components.

References

1. Albrecht, S.V., Stone, P.: Autonomous agents modelling other agents: a comprehensive survey and open problems. Artif. Intell. **258**, 66–95 (2018)
2. Allen, C., Smit, I., Wallach, W.: Artificial morality: top-down, bottom-up, and hybrid approaches. Ethics Inf. Technol. **7**(3), 149–155 (2005)
3. Batusov, V., Soutchanski, M.: Situation calculus semantics for actual causality. In: Proceedings of the AAAI Conference on Artificial Intelligence, vol. 32 (2018)
4. Belle, V., Papantonis, I.: Principles and practice of explainable machine learning. arXiv preprint arXiv:2009.11698 (2020)
5. Brachman, R.J., Levesque, H.J., Reiter, R.: Knowledge Representation. MIT Press (1992)
6. Broeck, G.V.D., Thon, I., Otterlo, M.V., Raedt, L.D.: DTProbLog: a decision-theoretic probabilistic prolog. In: Proceedings of the Twenty-Fourth AAAI Conference on Artificial Intelligence, AAAI 2010, pp. 1217–1222. AAAI Press (2010)
7. Choi, Y., Dang, M., Broeck, G.V.D.: Group fairness by probabilistic modeling with latent fair decisions. arXiv preprint arXiv:2009.09031 (2020)
8. Chouldechova, A.: Fair prediction with disparate impact: a study of bias in recidivism prediction instruments. Big Data **5**(2), 153–163 (2017)
9. Cozman, F.G., Munhoz, H.N.: Some thoughts on knowledge-enhanced machine learning. Int. J. Approximate Reasoning **136**, 308–324 (2021)
10. Crawford, K.: The Atlas of AI. Yale University Press, New Haven (2021)

11. Crawford, K.: The hidden costs of AI. New Sci. **249**(3327), 46–49 (2021)
12. Darwiche, A.: Causal inference using tractable circuits. arXiv preprint arXiv:2202.02891 (2022)
13. Dignum, V.: Responsible Artificial Intelligence: How to Develop and Use AI in a Responsible Way. Springer, Cham (2019). https://doi.org/10.1007/978-3-030-30371-6
14. Doshi-Velez, F., et al.: Accountability of AI under the law: the role of explanation. arXiv preprint arXiv:1711.01134 (2017)
15. Etzioni, A., Etzioni, O.: Incorporating ethics into artificial intelligence. J. Ethics **21**(4), 403–418 (2017)
16. Fagin, R., Moses, Y., Halpern, J.Y., Vardi, M.Y.: Reasoning About Knowledge. MIT Press, Cambridge (2003)
17. Farnadi, G., Babaki, B., Getoor, L.: Fairness in relational domains. In: Proceedings of the 2018 AAAI/ACM Conference on AI, Ethics, and Society, pp. 108–114 (2018)
18. Fierens, D., Van den Broeck, G., Thon, I., Gutmann, B., De Raedt, L.: Inference in probabilistic logic programs using weighted CNF's. In: Proceedings of UAI, pp. 211–220 (2011)
19. Friedler, S.A., Scheidegger, C., Venkatasubramanian, S.: On the (IM) possibility of fairness. arXiv preprint arXiv:1609.07236 (2016)
20. Ghaderi, H., Levesque, H., Lespérance, Y.: Towards a logical theory of coordination and joint ability. In: Proceedings of the 6th International Joint Conference on Autonomous Agents and Multiagent Systems, pp. 1–3 (2007)
21. Halpern, J.Y.: Actual Causality. MIT Press, Cambridge (2016)
22. Halpern, J.Y.: Reasoning About Uncertainty. MIT Press, Cambridge (2017)
23. Hammond, L., Belle, V.: Learning tractable probabilistic models for moral responsibility and blame. Data Min. Knowl. Disc. **35**(2), 621–659 (2021). https://doi.org/10.1007/s10618-020-00726-4
24. Kambhampati, S.: Challenges of human-aware AI systems. AI Mag. **41**(3), 3–17 (2020)
25. Khandani, A., Kim, J., Lo, A.: Consumer credit-risk models via machine-learning algorithms. J. Bank. Finan. **34**, 2767–2787 (2010)
26. Papantonis, I., Belle, V.: Interventions and counterfactuals in tractable probabilistic models. In: NeurIPS Workshop on Knowledge Representation & Reasoning Meets Machine Learning (2019)
27. Papantonis, I., Belle, V.: Closed-form results for prior constraints in sum-product networks. Frontiers Artif. Intell. **4**, 644062 (2021)
28. Papantonis, I., Belle, V.: Principled diverse counterfactuals in multilinear models. arXiv preprint arXiv:2201.06467 (2022)
29. Rudin, C.: Stop explaining black box machine learning models for high stakes decisions and use interpretable models instead. Nat. Mach. Intell. **1**(5), 206–215 (2019)
30. Salimi, B., Parikh, H., Kayali, M., Getoor, L., Roy, S., Suciu, D.: Causal relational learning. In: Proceedings of the 2020 ACM SIGMOD International Conference on Management of Data, pp. 241–256 (2020)
31. Sardina, S., De Giacomo, G., Lespérance, Y., Levesque, H.J.: On the limits of planning over belief states under strict uncertainty. In: KR vol. 6, pp. 463–471 (2006)
32. Stilgoe, J.: Machine learning, social learning and the governance of self-driving cars. Soc. Stud. Sci. **48**(1), 25–56 (2018)
33. Varley, M., Belle, V.: Fairness in machine learning with tractable models. Knowl. Based Syst. **215**, 106715 (2021)

34. Zanzotto, F.M.: Human-in-the-loop artificial intelligence. J. Artif. Intell. Res. **64**, 243–252 (2019)
35. Zečević, M., Dhami, D., Karanam, A., Natarajan, S., Kersting, K.: Interventional sum-product networks: causal inference with tractable probabilistic models. In: Advances in Neural Information Processing Systems, vol. 34 (2021)

Modelling and Knowledge Representation

Scrutable Robot Actions Using a Hierarchical Ontological Model

Martin Jedwabny[1(✉)], Pierre Bisquert[1,2], and Madalina Croitoru[1]

[1] LIRMM, Inria, Univ Montpellier, CNRS, Montpellier, France
{martin.jedwabny,madalina.croitoru}@lirmm.fr
[2] IATE, Univ Montpellier, INRAE, Institut Agro, Montpellier, France
pierre.bisquert@inrae.fr

Abstract. We place ourselves in the context of representing knowledge inside the cognitive model of a robot that needs to reason about its actions. We propose a new ontological transformation system able to model different levels of knowledge granularity. This model will allow to unfold the sequences of actions the robot performs for better scrutability.

Keywords: Reasoning about action · Ontology · Scrutability

1 Introduction

In this paper, we present a formal approach to knowledge representation and reasoning in the setting of a robot making decisions about which action to perform. We propose a hierarchical structure to examine information about actions in depth, by unfolding actions into several layers of complexity. The intuition of this work relies on ideas from episodic memory theory [1], that organizes information in layers of detail retrievable at the right time, in the right granularity.

We propose a hierarchical information structure composed by two combinatorial structures that can be applied in an Artificial Intelligence (AI) planning [17] setting: (i) an ontology of fluent and action symbols, and (ii) a hierarchical structure encoding preconditions and effects for the various actions.

The proposed layered catalog of actions is influenced by work on conceptual graph-based ontological knowledge representation [18]. This work can be seen as a continuation of previous work on hierarchical conceptual graphs [11], with a focus on reasoning about action.

The salient points of the paper are the following:

- A knowledge representation model relevant for ontologies of fluents and actions, and
- A formal method for translating between the different layers of details corresponding to these ontologies.

After providing a motivating example in Sect. 2, we recall in Sect. 3 the necessary notions for graphical knowledge representation. In Sect. 4 we introduce

T. Braun et al. (Eds.): ICCS 2022, LNCS 13403, pp. 11–24, 2022.
https://doi.org/10.1007/978-3-031-16663-1_2

the structures that allow to represent the robot's knowledge about the world and its possible actions. Section 5 analyses the related work and discusses ways in which our framework can be used to make a planner more scrutable for an user. Finally, we will conclude in Sect. 6.

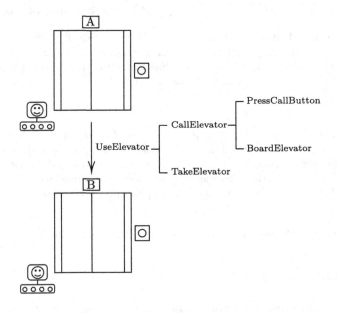

Fig. 1. Elevator example illustration

2   Motivating Example

Consider a situation in which a robot has to board an elevator in a building to get from floor f_A to f_B. An action model of the situation might represent this as a single action $UseElevator$ that, upon execution, takes a situation in which the robot is in f_A and transforms it in such a way the robot goes to f_B. Modeling the action of using the elevator as a single atomic step comes with the immediate advantage of compactness.

However, in certain cases the elevator could malfunction due to electricity shortages, a certain button not working, or any other internal or external factor that disturbs its normal functioning. In this case, the robot could perceive that the action $UseElevator$ is no longer producing its intended result, but would have a hard time realizing the cause without modeling the state of the electricity in the building. On the other hand, keeping track of this property might be irrelevant to actions other than $UseElevator$ and make it harder to a user to understand the model and sequence of actions chosen by the robot if many other properties are introduced.

Upon closer inspection, we realize that the action *UseElevator* depends on many factors like the state of electricity, the buttons used to operate the elevator and the electronic circuit that receives the button's signal. Furthermore, the action can be broken down to several steps, as depicted in Fig. 1: (i) *CallElevator* using button b_A from whichever floor it is currently at to f_A, and (ii) *TakeElevator* by selecting the destination floor f_B with selector button b_B. Then, (i) can also be separated into two actions: *PressCallButton*, and *BoardElevator*. In the same way, these actions can be iteratively broken down into several layers of increasing complexity.

Nevertheless, from a user point of view, all of these factors and step breakdown could be irrelevant in correct operation circumstances. Both for a monitoring user and a automatic planning robot, it can be useful to take these multiple levels of model complexity into account and use them only when they are needed.

3   Background Notions

3.1   Bipartite Graphs

A *bipartite graph* is a graph $G = (V_G, E_G)$ with the nodes set $V_G = V_F \cup V_A$, where V_F and V_A are finite disjoint sets, and each edge $e \in E_G$ is a two-element set $e = \{v_F, v_A\}$, where $v_F \in V_F$ and $v_A \in V_A$. Usually, a bipartite graph G is denoted as $G = (V_F, V_A, E_G)$. We call $G^\emptyset$ the empty bipartite graph without nodes and edges.

We make the informal observation that, later on in the paper, the node set V_F and V_A will be used to represent, respectively, the uninstanced fluent (i.e., the description of a scene) and action symbols of the planning setting. Edges in the bipartite graph will thus capture the preconditions and effects, in terms of fluents that compose an action.

Let $G = (V_F, V_A, E_G)$ be a bipartite graph. The number of edges incident to a node $v \in V(G)$ is the degree, $d_G(v)$, of the node v. If, for each $v_A \in V_A$ there is a linear order $e_1 = \{v_A, v_1\}, \ldots, e_k = \{v_A, v_k\}$ on the set of edges incident to v_A (where $k = d_g(v)$), then G is called an *ordered bipartite graph*. A simple way to express that G is ordered is to provide a labelling $l : E_G \mapsto \{1, \ldots, |V_F|\}$ with $l(\{v_A, w\})$ the index of the edge $\{v_A, w\}$ in the above ordering of the edges incident in G to v_A. l is called a *order labelling* of the edges of G. We denote an ordered bipartite graph by $G = (V_F, V_A, E_G, l)$. It will be useful for the next sections to note that the labelling l can be generalized into a collection of labellings of different kinds by extending its definition to $l : E_G \mapsto 2^{K \times \{1, \ldots, |V_F|\}} - \{\emptyset\}$ with K a predefined set of kinds, while still being trivial to construct an overall labelling $l' : E_G \mapsto \{1, \ldots, |V_F|\}$ from it.

For a vertex $v \in V_F \cup V_A$, the symbol $N_G(v)$ denotes its neighbors set, i.e. $N_G(v) = \{w \in V_F \cup V_A | \{v, w\} \in E_G\}$. Similarly, if $A \subseteq V_A \cup V_F$, the set of its neighbors is $N_G(A) = \cup_{v \in A} N_G(v) - A$. If G is an ordered bipartite graph, then for each $r \in V_A$, the symbol $N_G^i(r)$ denotes the i-th neighbor of r, i.e. $v = N_G^i(r)$ if and only if $\{r, v\} \in E_G$ and $l(\{r, v\}) = i$.

Throughout this paper we use a particular type of subgraph of a bipartite graph: $G^1 = (V_F^1, V_A^1, E_G^1)$ is a subgraph of $G = (V_F, V_A, E_G)$ if $V_F^1 \subseteq V_F$, $V_A^1 \subseteq V_A$, $N_G(V_A^1) \subseteq V_F^1$ and $E_G^1 = \{ \{v, w\} \in E_G | v \in V_F^1, w \in V_A^1 \}$. In other words, we require that the (ordered) set of all edges incident in G to a vertex from V_A^1 must appear in G^1. Therefore, a subgraph is completely specified by its vertex set. In particular, if $A \subseteq V_F$:

- The *subgraph spanned by* A *in* G, denoted as $\lceil A \rceil^G$, has $V_F(\lceil A \rceil^G) = A \cup N_G(N_G(A))$ and $V_A(\lceil A \rceil^G) = N_G(A)$.
- The *subgraph generated by* A *in* G, denoted as $\lfloor A \rfloor_G$, has $V_F(\lfloor A \rfloor_G) = A$ and $V_A(\lfloor A \rfloor_G) = \{v \in N_G(A) | N_G(v) \subseteq A\}$.
- For $A \subseteq V_A$, *the subgraph induced by* A *in* G, denoted $[A]_G$, has $V_F([A]_G) = N_G(A)$ and $V_A([A]_G) = A$.

Now that we can represent the links between actions and fluents as a graph, we will see in the following section how we can define the types of their arguments.

3.2 Planning

We will use an abstract representation inspired by the one in [5] to model belief state planning. This representation allows to model non-deterministic/belief states and deterministic actions with conditional effects, i.e., conformant planning.

It is assumed that one is given a set of *fluents* $F_\mathcal{P}$ and *actions* $A_\mathcal{P}$, denoting the properties of a problem and the actions the agent can perform, respectively. A *literal* is either $f \in F_\mathcal{P}$ a fluent, or $\neg f$ its negation. A *state* $s \subseteq F_\mathcal{P}$ is a set of fluents denoting what properties hold in a state. This takes into account the closed-world assumption, in that all fluents that are not in a state are assumed to be false. A *belief state* $B \subseteq 2^{F_\mathcal{P}}$ is a set of states.

An action $a \in A_\mathcal{P}$ is of the form $a = (pre(a), eff(a))$, where $pre(a)$ is a set of literals over $F_\mathcal{P}$ called the *preconditions*. Then, $eff(a) = \{eff_1(a), \ldots, eff_n(a)\}$ is a set of *effects* of the form $eff_i(a) = cond_i(a) \rightarrow post_i(a)$, where $cond_i(a)$ and $post_i(a)$ are sets of literals called *condition* and *postcondition*, respectively. We say that a set of literals L over $F_\mathcal{P}$ is compatible with a state $s \subseteq F_\mathcal{P}$, denoted $compat(L, s)$, when $\forall f \in F_\mathcal{P}$ it holds that $f \in L \Rightarrow f \in s$ and $\neg f \in L \Rightarrow f \notin s$. An action $a \in A_\mathcal{P}$ is applicable in state $s \subseteq F_\mathcal{P}$, denoted $applicable(a, s)$, if and only if $compat(pre(a), s)$ holds. Similarly, given a belief state $B \subseteq 2^{F_\mathcal{P}}$, $applicable(a, B)$ holds if and only if $\forall s \in B$ it is the case that $applicable(a, s)$ is true.

If an action a is applicable in state s, the successor state, i.e., the state that results from performing a in s, is defined as $succ(a, s) = (s - \{f \in F_\mathcal{P} : \exists i \text{ s.t. } \neg f \in post_i(a) \text{ and } compat(cond_i(a), s)\}) \cup \{f \in F_\mathcal{P} : \exists i \text{ s.t. } f \in post_i(a) \text{ and } compat(cond_i(a), s)\}$. The successor to a belief state $B \subseteq 2^{F_\mathcal{P}}$ is defined as $succ(a, B) = \bigcup_{s \in B} succ(a, s)$.

A sequence of actions $\pi = [a_0, a_1, \ldots, a_n]$ where $n \in \mathbb{N}_0$ and $a_i \in A_\mathcal{P}$ is applicable to belief state $B \subseteq 2^{F_\mathcal{P}}$, denoted $applicable(\pi, B)$ if and only if either

$n = 0$, or otherwise $applicable(a_0, B)$ and $applicable([a_1, \ldots, a_n], succ(a_0, B))$ hold. If $applicable(\pi, B)$ does indeed hold, then $succ(\pi, B) = B$ if $n = 0$, otherwise $succ(\pi, B) = succ([a_1, \ldots, a_n], succ(a_0, B))$.

A *planning problem* is a tuple $\mathcal{P} = (F_\mathcal{P}, A_\mathcal{P}, I_\mathcal{P}, G_\mathcal{P})$:

- $F_\mathcal{P}$ is a set of fluents,
- $A_\mathcal{P}$ is a set of actions over $F_\mathcal{P}$,
- $I_\mathcal{P} \subseteq 2^{F_\mathcal{P}}$ is a non-empty set of states called the initial belief state, and
- $G_\mathcal{P} \subseteq 2^{F_\mathcal{P}}$ is a non-empty set of states called the goal.

A sequence π of actions is a *strong plan*, i.e., a solution that always reaches the goal, when $succ(\pi, I_\mathcal{P}) \subseteq G_\mathcal{P}$. Less restrictive, π is a *weak plan*, i.e., a sequence that sometimes reaches the goal, when $\exists s \in succ(\pi, I_\mathcal{P})$ such that $s \in G_\mathcal{P}$.

We refer the reader to [2,5,9] for results on the complexity and heuristics methods to generate strong and weak plans for a planning model such as the one described here.

4 Layered Catalog Graphs

Influenced by episodic memory theory [1], the knowledge of an agent is defined by two combinatorial structures.

- On one hand, we will consider an ontology of fluent and action symbols. The fluent symbols (represented by unary concepts) are organized in a type hierarchy. Similarly, the action symbols, represented by binary or n-ary relations are also organized in a relation hierarchy. The action symbols have a signature of their arguments, represented as fluent concept types.
- On the other hand, the agent will dispose of a hierarchical structure encoding preconditions and effects for various actions.

We only consider unary fluents for simplification purposes, however it is immediate to see how we could extend this work in order to consider fluents of any arity.

Let us note that the following definitions 1–7 are based on previous work on conceptual graphs [11], although adapted to represent fluents and actions instead of abstract concepts. Moreover, the framework presented in this paper could not be modeled as-is with the mentioned literature due to the way in which multiple fluents can relate to actions as preconditions and effects at the same time.

The ontology is defined as follows:

Definition 1. *An ontology is a 4-tuple $S = (T_F, T_A, \mathcal{I}, *)$ where:*

- *T_F is a finite partially ordered set (poset) $(T_F, \leq)$ of fluent types, defining a type hierarchy which has a greatest element $\top_C$, namely the universal type. In this specialization hierarchy, $\forall x, y \in T_F$ the symbolism $x \leq y$ is used to denote that x is a subtype of y.*

- T_A is a finite set of action types partitioned into k posets $(T_A^i, \leq)_{i=1,k}$ of relation types of arity i $(1 \leq i \leq k)$, where k is the maximum arity of an action type in T_A. Moreover, each action type of arity i, $r \in T_A^i$, has an associated signature $\sigma(r) \in \underbrace{T_F \times \ldots \times T_F}_{i \ times}$, which specifies the maximum fluent type of each of its arguments. This means that if we use $r(x_1, \ldots, x_i)$, then x_j is a fluent with $type(x_j) \leq \sigma(r)_j$ $(1 \leq j \leq i)$, where type is the function that returns the type of a fluent. The partial orders on relation types of the same arity must be signature-compatible, i.e., it must be such that $\forall r_1, r_2 \in T_A^i \ r_1 \leq r_2 \Rightarrow \sigma(r_1) \leq \sigma(r_2)$.
- $\mathcal{I}$ is a countable set of individual markers, used represent to given constants.
- $*$ is the generic marker to denote an unspecified fluent (with a known type).
- The sets T_F, T_A, $\mathcal{I}$ and $\{*\}$ are mutually disjoint and $\mathcal{I} \cup \{*\}$ is partially ordered by $x \leq y$ if and only if $x = y$ or $y = *$, for any given $x, y \in \mathcal{I} \cup \{*\}$.

It is worth to notice that the generic marker '$*$' will be used in this framework to represent variables/un-instanced concepts in the arguments of fluents and actions later.

The following depicts an ontology for the situation described before:

Example 1 (Elevator continued). We specify the types of fluents and actions as:

- $T_F = \{Button, Floor, \top_C\}$, the fluent types, where $Button, Floor \leq \top_C$ are the only subtypes,
- $T_A = \{UseElevator^T\}$, the action types, where $\sigma(UseElevator^T) = (Button, Button, Floor, Floor)$.
- $\mathcal{I} = \{b_A, b_B, f_A, f_B\}$, individuals.

As we can see, the ontology provides a support of types for fluents and actions. In this case, we represent a basic action type for pressing the elevator button that has a signature composed of elements of type *Button* and of type *Floor*, corresponding to the arguments of such an action.

For the representation of the hierarchical knowledge of the agent we define a simple graphical catalog of actions (SC) with their preconditions and effects. The simple graph catalog is rendered hierarchical by a transformation called transitional description defined further in the paper. The result will be a layered graphical catalog of actions (LC) that the robot can access according to the need at hand.

A SC provides a semantic set of pointers to the ontology of fluents and action symbols.

Definition 2. *A simple graphical catalog of actions is a 3-tuple $SC = [S, G, \lambda]$, where:*

- $S = (T_F, T_A, \mathcal{I}, *)$ *is the ontological support,*

- $G = (V_F, V_A, E_G, l)$ is an ordered bipartite graph, where V_F are called fluent symbols and V_A action symbols,
- l is a labelling that maps each edge $\{v_A, v_F\} \in E_G$ to a non-empty set of pairs $(k, i) \in l(\{v_A, v_F\})$ where $i \in \{1, \ldots, d_G(v_A)\}$ and k is either pre^+, pre^-, $cond_j^+$, $cond_j^-$, $post_j^+$, or $post_j^-$, with $j \in \mathbb{N}_{>0}$, denoting whether v_F is a positive or negative literal in the precondition, jth effect condition, or jth effect postcondition of v_A.
- λ is a labelling of the nodes of G with elements from the support S:
  $\forall r \in V_A, \ \lambda(r) \in T_A^{n_A}$ such that $n_A \in \mathbb{N}_{>0}$;
  $\forall c \in V_F, \ \lambda(c) \in T_F \times (\mathcal{I} \cup \{*\})$ such that
  if $c = N_G^i(r)$, $\lambda(r) = t_r$ and $\lambda(c) = (t_c, ref_c)$, then $t_c \leq \sigma(t_r)_i$.

Intuitively, λ allows to make the link between nodes in G that represent fluent and action symbols, and their respective types defined in S. Moreover, the labelling allows to denote that a fluent is a precondition and/or effect of an action. Let us depict the meaning of λ and l with the following example.

Example 2 (Elevator continued). Having defined an ontological support $S = (T_F, T_A, \mathcal{I}, *)$, we can instantiate a simple graphical catalog of actions $SC = [S, G, \lambda]$ by specifying $G = (V_F, V_A, E_G, l)$ and λ as follows:

- $V_F = \{InFloorElevator, InFloorAgent, CanUseCallButton, CanUseSelectButton\}$, the set of fluent symbols, where
  $\lambda(InFloorElevator) = (*, Floor)$,
  $\lambda(InFloorAgent) = (*, Floor)$,
  $\lambda(CanUseCallButton) = (*, Button)$,
  $\lambda(CanUseSelectButton) = (*, Button)$.
- $V_A = \{UseElevator\}$, the set of action symbols, where $\lambda(UseElevator) = UseElevator^T$.
- $E_G = \{\{UseElevator, X\} : X \in \{InFloorElevator, InFloorAgent, CanUseCallButton, CanUseSelectButton\}\}$,
- l the labelling assigns
  $l(\{UseElevator, CanUseCallButton\}) = \{(cond_1^+, 1)\}$,
  $l(\{UseElevator, CanUseSelectButton\}) = \{(cond_1^+, 2)\}$,
  $l(\{UseElevator, InFloorAgent\}) = \{(pre^+, 3), (post_1^+, 4), (post_1^-, 3)\}$,
  $l(\{UseElevator, InFloorElevator\}) = (post_1^+, 4)$.

We can see the SC $[S, G, \lambda]$ in Fig. 2. The fluent symbols in V_F are mapped by λ to the generic marker '*' to denote that they refer to a variable and not a specific constant. In particular, the symbol $InFloorElevator$ represents the current floor of the elevator, $InFloorAgent$ the floor of the agent, $CanUseCallButton$ whether the agent can use the button to call the elevator, and $CanUseSelectButton$ the same for the button inside the elevator. The action symbol $UseElevator$ has type $UseElevator^T$ with signature $\sigma(UseElevator) = (Button, Button, Floor, Floor)$. This will be used to characterize the type of the arguments of the (instanced) action. Then, a label $l(\{UseElevator, v_F\}) = (k, i)$ denotes that the ith argument of

$UseElevator$ corresponds to the (unique) argument of the fluent v_F, while k represents the role of the fluent in the action. As we will see later, such an action will get translated in our planning framework to something similar to an action $UseElevator(x, y, z, w) = (\{InFloorAgent(z)\}, \{cond_1 \rightarrow eff_1\})$, where $cond_1 = \{CanUseCallButton(x), CanUseSelectButton(y)\}$ and $eff_1 = \{InFloorAgent(w), \neg InFloorAgent(z), InFloorElevator(w)\}$.

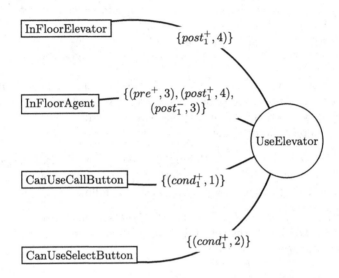

Fig. 2. Bipartite graph for the action symbol $UseElevator$

Transitional descriptions will allow for the definition of layered catalogs, which represent the different levels of complexity in which we can break down the model. Briefly, they represent a single step of expansion of action and fluents into a new layer of complexity. A transitional description $\mathcal{TD}$ contains a collection of bipartite graphs for each node of the original bipartite graph G that one wants to expand, which represent the new added knowledge. Let us now define what is a transitional description for a graph.

Definition 3. *Let* $G = (V_F, V_A, E_G)$ *be a bipartite graph. A transitional description associated to G is a pair $\mathcal{TD} = (D, (G.d)_{d \in D \cup N_G(D)})$ where*

- $D \subseteq V_F$ *is a set of complex fluent symbols, i.e.: a subset of the original fluents symbols in V_F that can be expanded into a more complex representation.*
- *For each $d \in D \cup N_G(D)$ $G.d$ is a bipartite graph.*
- *If $d \in D$ then $G.d$ is the non-empty ($G.d \neq G^{\emptyset}$) description of the complex fluent symbol d. Distinct complex fluent symbols $d, d' \in D$ have disjoint descriptions $G.d \cap G.d' = G^{\emptyset}$.*
- *If $d \in N_G(D)$ then $G.d \neq G^{\emptyset}$, $N_G(d) - D \subseteq V_F(G.d)$ and $V_F(G.d) \cap V_F(G.d') \neq \emptyset$ if and only if $d' \in N_G(d) \cap D$.*

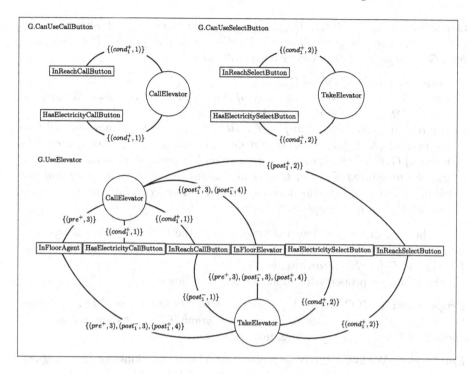

Fig. 3. Transitional description for the elevator example

Note that $(G.d)_{d \in D \cup N_G(D)}$ is the collection of bipartite graphs for each node d of the original bipartite graph that we want to expand. Moreover, when one expands a fluent symbol, so do the action symbols it is related to. Conversely, when an action symbol is expanded, the nodes in its expanded graph are the same as those in the expansion of its related complex fluent symbols, or its non-complex neighbors.

Let us illustrate this definition as follows.

Example 3 (Elevator continued). As we explained in Fig. 1, we would like to be able to separate the action symbol $UseElevator$ into two: $CallElevator$ and $TakeElevator$. We can do this by using a transitional description $\mathcal{TD} = (D, (G.d)_{d \in D \cup N_G(D)})$ as depicted in Fig. 3, where $D = \{CanUseCallButton, CanUseSelectButton\}$. Here, we see three SCs, namely '$G.CanUseCallButton$', '$G.CanUseSelectButton$' and '$G.CanUseElevator$'. While the first two represent the corresponding SCs obtained by augmenting the granularity of those fluents, the third one showcases the augmented version of the action '$UseElevator$', whose new level of granularity is obtained using the updated SCs of its fluents, all of which is generated with the transitional description $\mathcal{TD}$.

Finally let us now define how to apply a transitional description to a simple catalog to expand the representation.

Definition 4. *If $\mathcal{TD} = (D, (G.d)_{d \in D \cup N_G(D)})$ is a transitional description associated to the bipartite graph $G = (V_F, V_A, E_G)$, then the graph $\mathcal{TD}(G)$ obtained from G by applying $\mathcal{TD}$ is constructed as follows:*

1. *Take a new copy of $\lfloor V_F - D \rfloor_G$.*
2. *For each $d \in D$, take a new copy of the graph $G.d$ and make the disjoint union of it with the current graph constructed.*
3. *For each $d \in N_G(D)$, identify the nodes of $G.d$ which are already added to the current graph (i.e. the atomic nodes of G that are neighbors of d and the nodes of $G.d'$ which appear in $G.d$). For each complex neighbor d' of d in G, add the remaining nodes of $G.d$ as new nodes in the current graph and link all these nodes by edges as described in $G.d$ (in order to have an isomorphic copy of $G.d$ as a subgraph in the current graph).*

In the case of the previous example, due to the fact that there is only one action symbol in the catalog $[S, G, \lambda]$ defined previously, the bipartite graphs $\mathcal{TD}(G)$ and $G.UseElevator$ are identical.

The following property for bipartite graphs follows.

Proposition 1. *If $G = (V_F, V_A, E_G)$ is a bipartite graph and $\mathcal{TD}$ is a transitional description associated to G, then the graph $\mathcal{TD}(G)$ obtained from G by applying $\mathcal{TD}$ is also a bipartite graph.*

Proof sketch. We follow the construction given in the previous definition regarding the application of a transitional description $\mathcal{TD}$ to a bipartite graph G.

It is immediate to see that the starting graph in (1) $\lfloor V_F - D \rfloor_G$ is a bipartite one because G was bipartite. Then for point (2), each expanded graph $G.d$ is a bipartite one by definition and by applying a disjoint union with another bipartite graph, the property is preserved. Finally, point (3) only links fluent nodes to actions nodes, which also preserves the bipartite property.   □

This proposition ensures that the graph obtained by applying the transitional description can itself be expanded using another.

So far, our definition of transitional description only accounts for nodes and actions, but not that their expansions match their types, when considering ontological supports. The following definition extends the notion for a simple graphical catalog of actions to account for the types of fluents and actions.

Definition 5. *Let $SC = [S, G, \lambda]$ be a graphical catalog of actions, where $G = (V_F, V_A, E_G, l)$. A transitional description associated to SC is a pair $\mathcal{TD} = (D, (SC.d)_{d \in D \cup N_G(D)})$ where:*

- *$D \subseteq V_F$ is a set of complex fluent symbols.*
- *For each $d \in D \cup N_G(D)$, $SC.d = [S.d, G.d, \lambda.d]$ is a SC.*
- *If $d \in D$, then $G.d$ is the non-empty ($G.d \neq G^{\emptyset}$) description of the complex fluent symbol d. Distinct complex fluent symbols $d, d' \in D$ have disjoint descriptions $G.d \cap G.d' = G^{\emptyset}$. Moreover, for all $v \in V_F(G.d)$, it holds that $\lambda(d) = \lambda.d(v)$.*

– If $d \in N_G(D)$, then $G.d \neq G^\emptyset$, $N_G(d) - D \subseteq V_F(G.d)$, and $V_F(G.d) \cap V_F(G.d') \neq \emptyset$ for each $d' \in N_G(d) \cap D$. Moreover, $S.d \supseteq S \cup_{d' \in N_G(d)} S.d'$, $\lambda.d(v) = \lambda(v)$ for $v \in N_G(d) - D$ and $\lambda.d(v) = \lambda.d'(v)$ for $v \in V_F(G.d) \cap V_F(G.d')$. Finally, for each $d' \in V_A(G.d)$, it holds that $\lambda(d) = \lambda.d(d')$, i.e., when decomposing an action through a transitional description, the corresponding actions preserve its type.

Note that we disallow $G.d = G^\emptyset$, as this would erase the node when applying a transitional description. In the simplest case, the new graph can only be composed of the original node itself, thus not producing any changes.

Analogously to the extension of transitional descriptions from bipartite graphs to SCs, the following definition extends the *application* of a TD, to take into account the types.

Definition 6. *If* $TD = (D, (SC.d)_{d \in D \cup N_G(D)})$ *is a transitional description associated to* $SC = [S, G, \lambda]$, *then the simple graphical catalog of actions* $TD(SC)$ *obtained from* SC *by applying* TD *is* $TD(SC) = [S', TD(G), \lambda']$. *Here,* $TD(G)$ *is the bipartite graph* $TD(G)$ *obtained from* G *by applying* TD, $S' = \cup_{d \in D \cup N_G(D)} S.d$ *and* λ' *is any legal labelling function defined on* $V(TD(G))$ *which preserves the labels given to the vertices in* $V(G)$ *and* $V(G.d)$ *for all* $v \in D \cup N_G(D)$.

Note that the last condition in Definition 5 (concerning the preservation of types for the expanded action nodes) is the one that ensures that when expanding the nodes, the types coming from the ontologies will be preserved when applying a transitional description.

Moreover, using Proposition 1 we can verify that $TD(SC)$ is a simple graphical catalog of actions. This means that we can nest the application of transitional description to produce several expanded catalogs of actions of increasing complexity, which we define as follows:

Definition 7. *Let* n *be a non-negative integer. A layered catalog graph (LC) of depth* n *is a family* $\mathbf{LC} = \langle SC^0, TD^0, \ldots, TD^{n-1} \rangle$ *where:*

– $SC^0 = [S^0, (V_F^0, V_A^0, E^0), \lambda^0)]$ *is a* SC,
– TD^0 *is a transitional description associated to* SC^0,
– *for each* k, $1 \leq k \leq n - 1$, TD^k *is a transitional description associated to* $SC^k = [S^k, (V_F^k, V_A^k, E^k), \lambda^k)] = TD^{k-1}(SC^{k-1})$.

SC^0 *is the base simple graphical catalog of actions of the layered graph* $\mathbf{LC}$ *and* $SC^k = TD^{k-1}(SC^{k-1})$ $(k = 1, \ldots, n)$, *are its layers.*

In other words, if we have an interconnected world described by a SC and if we can provide details about both some complex fluent and action symbols, then we can construct a second level of knowledge about this world, describing these new details as graphs and applying the corresponding substitutions. This process can be similarly performed with the last constructed level, thus obtaining a coherent set of layered representations of the initial world.

5   Related Work

As we mentioned in the introduction, the motivation behind our work was to provide a mechanism that improved the scrutability of a planner for a human user.
Unfolding representations between multiple granularity levels has been studied
in the context of AI planning optimization [16] and generic conceptual graphs
[11], but not for scrutability and neither in such a way that fluents and actions
can be unfolded with the support of an ontology. In recent years, the AI planning community has taken interest in what in known as explainable AI planning
(XAIP) [14]. Notably, this branch has proposed several critical questions for AI
planners that can be of interest to human users: (i) why did you do that?, (ii)
why didn't you do something else?, (iii) why is what you propose to do more
efficient/safe/cheap than something else?, (iv) why can't you do that?, (v) why
do I need to replan at this point? and (vi) why do I not need to replan at this
point?. With that in mind, our framework could reinforce other techniques [7,8]
to provide an appropriate level of detail for the generated plan generated tailored
to a specific kind of user. At the same time, it could be applied in cases where
no plan can be generated by using counterfactuals [6,12], so that the planner
can iteratively inform the reason behind its failures.

Moreover, as far as we know, there is no work coupling structured hierarchical knowledge of fluents and actions in such a way that the robot can expand
sets of fluents to assess which action could be applied using a general abstract
graph-based ontology. Although our work extends previous literature for conceptual graphs [11], the mentioned literature would not allow to model action
preconditions and effects, due to the fact that the same fluent node cannot be
attached multiple times as one or the other, to the same action.

With regards to classical AI planning, our framework can be related to the
concept of 'macro operators' [4]. Macro operators were developed as an optimization technique for PDDL planners, which consists in learning operators (actions)
composed of several others before computing the plan for a complex task, based
on simpler ones. While this approach indeed allows to couple actions together,
this does not allow for several fluent granularity levels as we proposed here.

That being said, the proposed approach is related to the field of hierarchical
task networks (HTN) [13] where dependencies among actions can be structured
in the form of hierarchies linking actions to higher level compound ones. However,
this framework does not allow for the structured representation of knowledge we
provide. Some works have proposed ontologies for HTNs [15] domains, but not
with a focus on the transformation from one level of detail to another on the
fly as we do here. Similar to the macro operators, their work does not allow for
multiple fluent granularity levels and neither a mechanism to unfold them.

Perhaps closer to our work, hierarchical models for STRIPS-like planners
have been studied [16] as a method to improve the efficiency of plan generation
by mapping tasks to different granularity levels. In contrast to out framework,
this avenue of work focused on mapping fluent parameters, instead of fluent and
action symbols.

6   Conclusion

In this paper, we introduced a graph-based hierarchical model of knowledge about actions and fluents that allows to represent structured knowledge about the world under the form of increasingly detailed levels. We developed a graph-based framework supported by an ontology, called layered catalog of actions, to characterize an agent's actions. We showed how the fluents and actions of the framework can be specified using this catalog. Our work not only formalized this model, but also provided a method to adjust the level of detail of the fluents and actions using the concept of *transitional description*.

The proposed approach that joins structured and layered knowledge of actions opens different avenues of research for future work. In particular, by adapting the level of granularity, an agent could adapt to the level of understanding of the user. This could pave the way for robot-user explanation by task measurement, i.e., testing if the user can perform a task where multiple actions have to be performed after being exposed to an explanation by the robot of a similar problem.

Finally, because our framework relies on an ontology to represent the fluents of states and considers belief states, it could potentially allow for plausible reasoning [10] through the type of individuals. More precisely, when the properties of a certain individual are not fully known, it could be represented by using different beliefs about the types of that individual and then implementing plausible reasoning through the planner. In future work, this approach could also be extended to other kind of uncertainty, such as partial observability planning [3].

References

1. Baddeley, A.: The concept of episodic memory. Philos. Trans. R. Soc. London. Ser. B Biol. Sci. **356**(1413), 1345–1350 (2001)
2. Bonet, B., Geffner, H.: Planning with incomplete information as heuristic search in belief space. In: Proceedings of the Fifth International Conference on Artificial Intelligence Planning Systems, pp. 52–61 (2000)
3. Bonet, B., Geffner, H.: Planning under partial observability by classical replanning: theory and experiments. In: Twenty-Second International Joint Conference on Artificial Intelligence (2011)
4. Botea, A., Enzenberger, M., Müller, M., Schaeffer, J.: Macro-FF: Improving AI planning with automatically learned macro-operators. J. Artif. Intell. Res. **24**, 581–621 (2005)
5. Bryce, D., Kambhampati, S., Smith, D.E.: Planning graph heuristics for belief space search. J. Artif. Intell. Res. **26**, 35–99 (2006)
6. Byrne, R.M.: Counterfactuals in explainable artificial intelligence (XAI): Evidence from human reasoning. In: IJCAI, pp. 6276–6282 (2019)
7. Cashmore, M., Collins, A., Krarup, B., Krivic, S., Magazzeni, D., Smith, D.: Towards explainable AI planning as a service. arXiv preprint arXiv:1908.05059 (2019)
8. Chakraborti, T., Sreedharan, S., Kambhampati, S.: The emerging landscape of explainable AI planning and decision making. arXiv preprint arXiv:2002.11697 (2020)

9. Cimatti, A., Pistore, M., Roveri, M., Traverso, P.: Weak, strong, and strong cyclic planning via symbolic model checking. Artif. Intell. **147**(1–2), 35–84 (2003)
10. Collins, A., Michalski, R.: The logic of plausible reasoning: a core theory. Cogn. Sci. **13**(1), 1–49 (1989)
11. Croitoru, M., Compatangelo, E., Mellish, C.: Hierarchical knowledge integration using layered conceptual graphs. In: Dau, F., Mugnier, M.-L., Stumme, G. (eds.) ICCS-ConceptStruct 2005. LNCS (LNAI), vol. 3596, pp. 267–280. Springer, Heidelberg (2005). https://doi.org/10.1007/11524564_18
12. Das, D., Banerjee, S., Chernova, S.: Explainable AI for robot failures: generating explanations that improve user assistance in fault recovery. In: Proceedings of the 2021 ACM/IEEE International Conference on Human-Robot Interaction, pp. 351–360 (2021)
13. Erol, K., Hendler, J.A., Nau, D.S.: Semantics for hierarchical task-network planning. Maryland Univ College Park Inst for Systems Research, Technical Report (1995)
14. Fox, M., Long, D., Magazzeni, D.: Explainable planning. arXiv preprint arXiv:1709.10256 (2017)
15. Freitas, A., Schmidt, D., Meneguzzi, F., Vieira, R., Bordini, R.H.: Using ontologies as semantic representations of hierarchical task network planning domains. In: Proceedings of WWW, p. 124 (2014)
16. Galindo, C., Fernandez-Madrigal, J.A., Gonzalez, J.: Improving efficiency in mobile robot task planning through world abstraction. IEEE Trans. Robot. **20**(4), 677–690 (2004)
17. Ghallab, M., Nau, D., Traverso, P.: Automated Planning: theory and practice. Elsevier (2004)
18. Mugnier, M.L., Chein, M.: Conceptual graphs: fundamental notions. Revue d'intelligence artificielle **6**(4), 365–406 (1992)

TAQE: A Data Modeling Framework for Traffic and Air Quality Applications in Smart Cities

David Martínez[1] , Laura Po[2(✉)] , Raquel Trillo-Lado[3] ,
and José R.R. Viqueira[1]

[1] CiTIUS, University of Santiago de Compostela, Santiago de Compostela, Spain
{david.martinez.casas,jrr.viqueira}@usc.es
[2] University of Modena and Reggio Emilia, Modena, Italy
laura.po@unimore.it
[3] I3A, University of Zaragoza, Zaragoza, Spain
raqueltl@unizar.es

Abstract. Air quality and traffic monitoring and prediction are critical problems in urban areas. Therefore, in the context of smart cities, many relevant conceptual models and ontologies have already been proposed. However, the lack of standardized solutions boost development costs and hinder data integration between different cities and with other application domains. This paper proposes a classification of existing models and ontologies related to Earth observation and modeling and smart cities in four levels of abstraction, which range from completely general-purpose frameworks to application-specific solutions. Based on such classification and requirements extracted from a comprehensive set of state-of-the-art applications, TAQE, a new data modeling framework for air quality and traffic data is defined. The effectiveness of TAQE is evaluated both by comparing its expressiveness with the state-of-the-art of the same application domain and by its application in the "TRAFAIR – Understanding traffic flows to improve air quality" EU project.

Keywords: Conceptual modeling · Smart city · Environmental data · Air quality data · Traffic data

1 Introduction

In urban areas, traffic-related pollution is a crucial problem with high environmental impact since more than 40% of emissions of nitrogen oxides come from traffic. As air pollution entails damages on ecosystems, reducing pollutant emissions to the atmosphere is imperative. Environmental decision making in smart cities has to be based on sophisticated traffic and air quality monitoring

---

This research was funded by the TRAFAIR project (2017-EU-IA-0167), co-financed by the Connecting Europe Facility of the European Union.

and modeling infrastructures, which generate large amounts of data, which are complex both in structure and also in semantics [26].

Many specific data modeling solutions and ontologies are being used in different applications to represent such data in smart cities. The lack of a common standardized data modeling framework adds a critical barrier to the data integration [30,31] required for cross-city decision-making. Besides, and more importantly, it does not foster the reuse of conceptual modeling structures. Knowledge and data model reuse reduce development time and resources required for projects. Moreover, they also facilitate communication among the people involved in the information systems development process and in their maintenance. On the other hand, it has been shown that although a higher level of abstraction increases reusability, more specific models are more usable [18].

Based on the above, this paper defines TAQE, a conceptual modeling framework for the representation of air quality and traffic data generated by related smart city monitoring and modeling infrastructures. TAQE is embedded in an information architecture with four levels of abstraction, which is based on international standards of the Open Geospatial Consortium (OGC), the International Organization for Standardization (ISO) and the World Wide Web Consortium (W3C). The design of TAQE is based on a collection of requirements extracted from a comprehensive set of applications. The effectiveness of its data representation capabilities has been tested by two different means. First, TAQE and all the already existing models of a similar level of abstraction found in the literature were analyzed to check the fulfillment of the identified requirements. Second, TAQE was specialized to design the data model needed by the "TRAFAIR – Understanding traffic flows to improve air quality" EU project, to support the representation of its air quality, traffic observation and modeling data.

The paper is organized as follows. Section 2 analyzes well-know data models and ontologies useful in this context, defines the four-level information architecture considered in this proposal, and analyzes different use cases. Section 3 describes the set of requirements that air quality models and traffic models should meet. Section 4 and Sect. 5 are devoted to the definition of the proposed data modeling framework. The results of the evaluation of TAQE are shown in Sect. 6. Finally, some conclusions are presented in Sect. 7.

2   Data Models for Environmental Data and Smart Cities

Data models and semantics are a key aspect of the representation and enhancement of environmental and smart city data. This section classifies available data models into four levels of abstraction, starting from generic frameworks and data models and reaching specific applications.

2.1   Level 1: Data Modeling

A great amount of data infrastructures on the Web are based on Linked Open Data (LOD) best practices and Resource Description Framework (RDF)[1] to

---

[1] W3C RDF Prime: http://www.w3.org/TR/2004/REC-rdf-primer-20040210/.

facilitate information data integration and interoperability. The vocabularies used in RDF statements to identify objects and properties may also be defined in RDF with RDF Schema[2] primitives. The expressiveness of RDF Schema to define vocabularies is extended by the Web Ontology Language (OWL)[3].

So, at this level, several well-known general ontologies, such as the W3C Provenance Ontology (PROV-O), are considered relevant for traffic and air quality applications in smart cities. PROV-O allows representing provenance information (i.e., information about entities or organizations, activities and people involved in producing data), which can be used to form assessments about the quality, reliability or trustworthiness of the data produced in a variety of application domains by using the PROV Data Model[4], which has a modular design and three main entities: *Entity*, *Activity* and *Agent*. PROV Data Model considers entities and activities, and the time at which they were created, used, or ended; derivations of entities from other entities; and agents bearing responsibility for entities that were generated and activities that happened. Agents can form logical structures for their members.

2.2 Level 2: Earth Observation and Modeling and Smart Cities

Regarding sensor data widely used in Earth observation, the most popular ontology is the W3C Semantic Sensor Network Ontology (SSN) [10], which defines a vocabulary to describe sensors and their observations, including both observed values and required metadata of features of interest, observed properties, etc. SSN may be used to annotate sensors and observations, in a way aligned completely to the OGC and ISO Observations and Measurements (O&M) [11] standard, which provides a conceptual schema to represent the results of observation processes and the metadata of these processes, of the entities that are sampled by them (Features of Interest), and of the observation results obtained. Moreover, SSN is also aligned to the Extensible Observation Ontology (OBOE), and PROV Data Model considered in level 1 [21]. The lightweight core of SSN is the SOSA (Sensor Observation, Sample and Actuator) ontology. The core concepts or entities of SOSA are *Procedure*, *Sensor*, *ObservableProperty*, *Observation*, *FeatureOfInterest* and *Result*.

2.3 Level 3: Application Domains

At this level, we focus our attention on two related domains: Air Quality and Traffic Data.

Air Quality. Urban air pollution information is usually processed by specialists to monitor, predict, and study air pollution sources within the urban area. Several platforms display statistics or semi-real time air quality measures, like

---

[2] W3C RDF Schema: http://www.w3.org/TR/rdf-schema/.

[3] W3C OWL 2: https://www.w3.org/TR/owl2-overview/.

[4] PROV Data Model: https://www.w3.org/TR/prov-dm/.

World's Air Pollution: Real-time Air Quality Index[5] and Air quality statistics by European Environmental Agency (EEA)[6]. Air quality (AQ) monitoring is usually done using professional AQ monitoring stations; Environmental Agencies are in charge of analyzing AQ conditions and reporting the violations of the concentrations limits. In recent years, it has been explored the potential of low-cost environmental sensors for urban air pollution monitoring. Low-cost sensors can be placed in fixed positions or on vehicles or drones. Thus they can provide gases concentration in a location, on a path or in a 3D environment. Moreover, different studies have taken advantage of a variety of satellites to estimate different air emissions. On the other hand, air quality models are studied for the representation of observation data in the scope of air quality prediction applications. Air pollution modeling is a complex subject and is linked to 3D city models, meteorological elements, and air tainting information. 3D air pollution models and the associated simulation systems are those that aim at "reconstructing" the environment, its properties, and governing physical laws.

Several ontologies have been defined in a specific context to enrich the air quality measurements and simulations semantically. AIR_POLLUTION_Onto ontology [27] has been conceived for air pollution analysis and control in two case studies. Airbase is the European air quality dataset maintained by the EEA [17]. QBOAirbase, a provenance-augmented version of the Airbase dataset, is multidimensional dataset linked to the Semantic Web. hackAIR ontology has been created within the "hackAIR - Collective awareness platform for outdoor air pollution" EU project [32]. It can store observations from sensors, monitoring stations, AQ related values from fused or forecasted data, or from sky-depicted images, etc.

Models that are used for the study of air quality at an urban scale make use of a grid-based spatial resolution. An ontology of air quality models is defined in [25]. It is linked to 3D city models and other models related to sustainable development and urban planning. This ontology is devoted to representing pollutant dispersion in urban street canyons, a particular phenomenon that happens in some street bordered by buildings in a specific configuration.

Traffic Data. Traffic data plays a key role in a smart city, as enabling efficient transportation and sustainable mobility are important goals that allow enhancing the quality of life of citizens. Therefore, modeling traffic and sharing traffic data is very relevant for many cities [13,36]. Thanks to the collection and modeling of traffic data, public administrations can take informed decisions regarding mobility policies. Besides, offering traffic information to citizens can also help to raise awareness about the importance of choosing suitable mobility options to increase their well-being and reduce pollution. A wide range of different types of sensors can be used to measure traffic [20], such as inductive loops, microwave

---

[5] Real-time Air Quality Index: https://waqi.info/.
[6] Air quality statistics by EEA: https://www.eea.europa.eu/data-and-maps/dashboards/air-quality-statistics.

radars, and video image detection. On the other hand, traffic models are studied in order to simulate and predict traffic flows.

The Vocabulary to Represent Data About Traffic[7] has been proposed for the representation of the situation of traffic in a city. This vocabulary extends SSN [10] to represent the intensity of traffic in the different road segments of a city. In particular, it is used to represent road segments, traffic observations, sensor or sensing systems used to obtain a given measurement, the results of observations (which have values and are produced by a specific sensor or sensing system), and finally instances that represents the type of properties being measured. Authors of this work recommend using this vocabulary in conjunction with the vocabulary available on http://vocab.linkeddata.es/datosabiertos/def/urbanismo-infraestructuras/callejero in order to represent city road maps.

An Ontology Layer for Intelligent Transportation Systems in order to increase the traffic safety and improve the comfort of drivers is proposed in [16]. The ontology layer is composed of three groups of interrelated concepts: concepts related to vehicles, concepts related to roads, and concepts related to sensors. The concepts related to vehicles describe a taxonomy of vehicles of different types and also allow representing information about their routes and locations. The concepts related to the infrastructure include a taxonomy of different types of roads as well as the representation of other parts of the infrastructure, such as the road segments, traffic lights and traffic signs, lanes, road markings (e.g., painted arrows), tunnels, parkings, roundabouts, bridges, gas stations, and toll stations). Finally, the concepts related to sensors are based on the use of the SSN ontology. The previous work focuses on long-life elements of the roads, such as traffic signs or road segments, while in the open511 specification[8] and the Road Accident Ontology[9], special situations in roads, such as accidents, special events (e.g., a celebration of a sport event) or particular weather conditions and road conditions (e.g., snow, ice, or fire on the road), are considered.

2.4 Level 4: Use-Case Specific Applications

Several projects have exploited drones for AQ monitoring. Drones can quickly cover vast industrial or rural areas obtaining a complete and detailed pollution map of the target region [33]. From gases concentrations measured by drones real-time AQI maps in both 2D and 3D areas can be produced that describe the AQ conditions of an urban environment.

Sensors can also be placed on vehicles such as taxis or public transport vehicles. Sensors are anchored on top of vehicles, to create a mobile sensor network to increase the number of urban sites monitored. Graphs and heat maps to show an overview of the gasses levels on the taxis/bus routes can be created [22].

---

[7] http://vocab.linkeddata.es/datosabiertos/def/transporte/trafico.

[8] open511 specification: http://www.open511.org/.

[9] Road Accident Ontology: https://www.w3.org/2012/06/rao.html.

Satellite remote sensing of air quality has evolved drastically over the last decade. The satellite retrieved trace gases are useful in analyzing and forecasting events that affect air quality, and they can be used to the inference of surface air quality. Aerosol optical depth (AOD) derived from satellite remote sensing is widely used to estimate surface PM 2.5 concentrations. The satellite provides the total concentration of gases on the column between the surface and the top of the troposphere [23]. To provide an idea of their Spatio-temporal coverage, the ESA Sentinel-5P satellite has an orbital cycle of 16 days. Therefore, it can produce one value every 16 days for each location, around two values per month. Spatial resolution is quite low, above 5km, to be used at an urban scale.

The traditional methods used by public administrations for traffic monitoring are fixed measurement devices (such as inductive loop detectors, radars, video cameras, etc.) that collect data like vehicle presence, vehicle speed, vehicle length and class, vehicle presence, lane occupancy. However, these devices can only collect data on the specific section of the road where they are installed. The last few years have seen a dramatic increase in the presence of mobile or aerial devices. These devices have the advantage compared to detect detailed and accurate data over space and time and to cover a dynamic area. Smartphones are deemed valid for traffic sensing purposes since as long as there is a sufficient penetration rate, they will provide accurate measurements of the traffic flow (users with traffic sensors over the total cars which entered the target road should be at least 2–3%). Smartphones can provide location, altitude, and speed [24]. If the reported data from several users in each road segment at a given time interval are combined, a reasonable estimation of the traffic conditions can be obtained. Drones are used to monitor real-time traffic and also to detect speeding violations or congestion events [15]. They can identify the number of speeding violations, the average duration of the detected speeding violations, the number of congestion events: congestion events and the average period of the detected congestion events. Traffic models provide a representation of the road network in terms of the capacity it gives and the volume of traffic using it.

Traffic models are used to estimate the real traffic conditions in a city and to forecast the impact of policies that modify the viability or also forecast traffic predictions. A traffic model considers data coming from sensors and the traffic demand that can be represented through an Origin-Destination matrix for a different period (e.g., morning and evening peak hours). The output of a traffic model depends on the kind of model [14,19]. For macroscopic models, we have the density (or concentration), the flow (number of vehicles in an interval of time), and the speed. These parameters are expressed in average values.

3   Requirements for a Level 3 Air Quality and Traffic Data Modeling Framework

From the analysis of several specific applications, reported in Sect. 2.4, the following requirements for modeling air quality and traffic emerged.

A generic air quality data model has to provide support for:

A1 in-situ fixed devices (e.g. air quality station). An in-situ sensor collects data at a distance comparable or smaller than any linear dimension of the sensor.

A2 in-situ removable devices (e.g. low-cost air quality sensor). These devices can be moved in different locations, but they can measure at this point once they are in a static position.

A3 remote sensing infrastructures (e.g. those on-board of satellites). Remote sensing is the process of detecting and monitoring characteristics of an area by measuring them at a distance (typically from satellite or aircraft).

A4 ground mobile devices (e.g., AQ devices on buses, always at the same elevation). These devices provide in-situ data along a route.

A5 airborne mobile devices. They provide in-situ data through a 3D trajectory.

A6 in-situ sensors installed at various heights (e.g., application of sensors installed externally on a building on different floors).

A7 static models. Static models do not vary over time; they may be viewed as a "snapshot" of an ecosystem at a particular moment. An example of static air quality models are the interpolated real-time air quality maps that are created by interpolating sensor measurements.

A8 dynamic models. Dynamic models provide one means of simulating the time-dependent behavior of systems. Atmospheric dispersion models are dynamic models that use mathematical algorithms to simulate how pollutants in the atmosphere disperse and, in some cases, how they react.

The requirements for traffic data modelling are to support for:

T1 in-situ traffic observation. Similarly to **A1** and **A2**, these are traffic sensors located in a specific position.

T2 remote traffic observation at specific locations. Similarly to **A3**, these sensors may observe traffic at various locations at each time instant.

T3 static traffic models. Similarly to **A7**, a static model gives a snapshot of reality.

T4 dynamic traffic models. Similarly to **A8**, dynamic traffic models estimate the evolution concerning the time of traffic variables (flow intensity, occupancy, etc.) during a period.

4   Air Quality Model

The air quality data representation capabilities of the TAQE model are described below. The model specializes in the level 2 OGC O&M data model (grey color classes in subsequent figures) with feature (entity) and process types. The data types used to represent the geospatial characteristics of the involved entities are based on those proposed by OGC standards, including feature geometric data types[10] and temporal, spatial and spatio-temporal coverages[11]. The part of the model that represents the observed entities (features of interest in O&M notation) is depicted in Fig. 1.

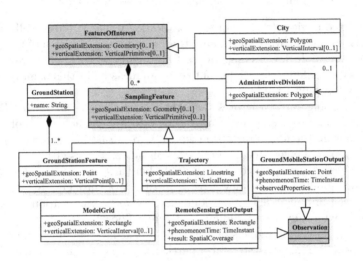

Fig. 1. Air quality feature of interest types in TAQE. (Grey background used to show types of the Level 2 OGC O&M data model).

Two subtypes of O&M *FeatureOfInterest* are considered, namely, *City* and *AdministrativeDivision*, to include respectively urban scale applications (smart city scope) and also applications at regional, national and international scale. Estimated properties are often generated at specific samples of the feature of interest (*SamplingFeature*). Various types of sampling features of interest in air quality observation and modeling are shown in Fig. 1, including locations of static and mobile ground stations, trajectories of flying platforms like drones and raster grids used by models and remote sensing platforms. Some of the sampling features are predefined, whereas others are generated by the observation or modeling processes; at the same time, they generate the observed property estimations. This is the case of ground mobile station features and remote sensing grids, which record both sampling features and property estimations, and therefore they inherit from both O&M *SamplingFeature* and O&M *Observation*. The remainder classes of the air quality model, i.e., those related to the representation of observation and modeling processes (O&M Process) and relevant outputs (O&M observation) are shown in Fig. 2. Data generation processes are

---

[10] OGC Simple Feature Access: https://www.opengeospatial.org/standards/sfa.
[11] OGC Coverage Implementation Schema: http://docs.opengeospatial.org/is/09-146r6/09-146r6.html.

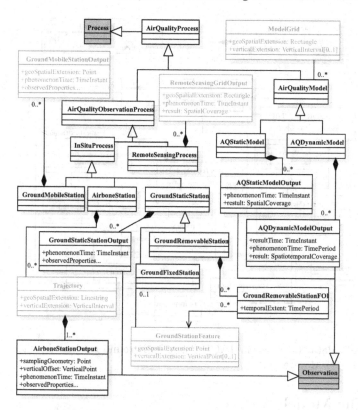

Fig. 2. Air quality process types in TAQE. (Grey background used to show types of the Level 2 OGC O&M data model. TAQE feature of interest types, already depicted in Fig. 1, are shown here in light-grey).

classified according to whether they observe or model properties. Based on the characteristics of their outputs, air quality models are further subdivided into static (*AQStaticModel*) and dynamic (*AQDynamicModel*). The former generates spatial coverages that estimate the observed properties at a specific time element (often real-time). In contrast, the latter provides spatio-temporal coverages that determine the evolution of those properties over a while. Air quality observation processes are also subdivided into in-situ (they observe in the surroundings of the process location) and remote sensing (they remotely observe all the places of an output spatial coverage at each time instant). In-situ processes are further classified into mobile ground stations (air quality stations installed in land vehicles), airborne stations (mounted on board of flying platforms such as drones) and ground static platforms, which are either air quality stations with a fixed location or air quality stations that may be installed at different locations during their lifetime.

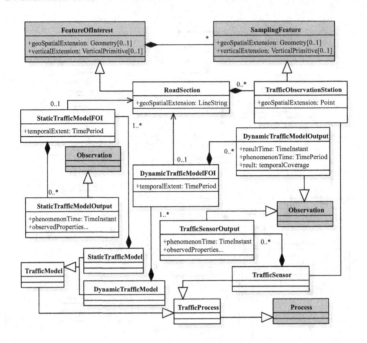

Fig. 3. Traffic data structures in TAQE (Grey background used to show types of the Level 2 OGC O&M data model).

5   Traffic Model

The data structures that enable TAQE to represent the results of traffic observation and modeling processes are graphically depicted in Fig. 3. Traffic data properties such as traffic speed, traffic flow intensity, and traffic occupancy are associated with sections of the road network in TAQE. Traffic models use to provide estimations (real-time estimations, future predictions, etc.) of the properties for a whole road section, whereas observation processes (*TrafficSensor*) use to perform their measures at specific sampling locations (*TrafficObservationStation*). As in the case of air quality, traffic models may be either static or dynamic (depending on whether they generate estimations for a specific temporal element or they generate an evolution concerning the time of the relevant properties).

6   Models Evaluation

The TAQE data modeling framework has been evaluated, both by testing its use in a specific application and by comparing its capabilities with already existing solutions of a similar level of abstraction.

6.1   Use Case

The "TRAFAIR - Understanding traffic flows to improve air quality" EU project (2017-EU-IA-0167) [29], funded by the Innovation and Networks Executive

Agency under its Connecting Europe Facility program, aims at building an urban scale air quality observation and modeling infrastructure at six cities of Italy and Spain. The main components of the infrastructure are: i) an air quality observation infrastructure based on low-cost sensors, ii) an air quality forecast service based on a lagrangian pollutant dispersion model, iii) a public open data infrastructure based on both OGC and W3C standards, connected to the European Data Portal through the involved public administrations and iv) specific web and mobile applications for public administrations and citizens.

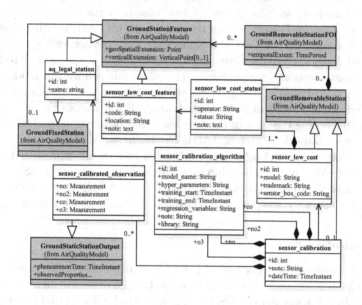

Fig. 4. Illustration of the specialization of TAQE in the TRAFAIR project (TAQE types shown in grey background).

To achieve the TRAFAIR objectives, both air quality and traffic have to be observed and modeled, and the relevant data has to be stored and published. Traffic sensors provide traffic flow intensity, average traffic speed, and traffic occupancy at specific locations of the road networks [3,4,12]. Erroneous measurements are detected and filtered out from the big data streams generated with appropriate techniques in near real-time [6,7]. Then, the observed traffic flow intensity is used as input by a static traffic flow model to estimate, in near real-time, the traffic flow intensity at each section of a subset of the city road network [2,5,28].

Regarding air quality, a network of removable low-cost sensors is used to perform measures at specific locations in each city [1,34,35]. Due to the characteristics of these low-cost devices, the quality of their measures disables their direct application. Intelligent regression models (sensor calibrations) are generated for each sensor, using the available ISO certified air quality stations as the ground truth. Those calibrations are next used to transform the voltages generated by the low-cost sensors to specific gas concentrations, enabling the use of these low-cost sensors at points where ISO stations are not located. In addition to the air quality observation, the traffic intensity at each road section, the meteorological conditions, and the city geometry (buildings) are used as input by a dynamic air quality model to generate 48-h air quality forecasts every day [8]. The use of TAQE to model all the above air quality and traffic data has been successfully tested. A short example of this testing is illustrated in Fig. 4, which shows how TAQE classes are specialized to model the air quality data generated by sensor calibrations. In particular, it is shown how TAQE *GroundStationFeature* is used to model both ISO certified air quality station locations (*aq_legal_station*) and removable low cost sensor locations (*sensor_low_cost_feature*). TAQE *GroundRemovableStation* is specialized to model both air quality sensors (*sensor_low_cost*) and sensor calibration models (*sensor_calibration*). Similarly, TAQE *GroundFixedStation* is specialized to model the set of devices installed in ISO certified air quality stations (*aq_legal_station*). Evolution concerning the time of the removable sensor locations and their status is modeled with a specialization of TAQE *GroundRemovableStationFOI*. Finally, the observations generated by sensor calibration models are represented by *sensor_calibrated_observation*, which inherits from TAQE *GroundStaticStationOutput*. All details of mappings between all the other TRAFAIR data structures and their TAQE abstract concepts are not given here due to space limitations.

6.2   Qualitative Evaluation

TAQE and previously proposed models for air quality and traffic representation defined in Sect. 2.3 have been evaluated w.r.t. the list of requirements defined in Sect. 3. Table 1 provide an overview of each model in level 3 related to air quality wrt requirements. While in Table 2 traffic models have been compared.

Table 1. Evaluation of the AQ models with respect to the requirements

Model	A1	A2	A3	A4	A5	A6	A7	A8
AIR_POLLUTION_Onto [27]	x	x	x					
QBOAirbase [17]	x	x	x				x	
Ontology of air quality models [25]							x	x
hackAIR ontology [32]	x	x	x			x	x	
TAQE model	x	x	x	x	x	x	x	x

AIR_POLLUTION_Onto supports in-situ and remote observations, but not models. QBOAirbase extends this view by also adding provenance; this might allow users to store static model outputs. Ontology of air quality models is devoted to representing only air quality models, while the hackAIR ontology integrates sensor measurements and air quality, models.

Table 2. Evaluation of the traffic models with respect to the requirements (p = partially, x = completely).

Model	T1	T2	T3	T4
Vocabulary to Represent Data About Traffic	x	x	x	
Ontology Layer for Intelligent Transportation [16]	x		x	
open511 specification				
Road Accident Ontology				
TAQE model	p		x	x

The model considered in the Vocabulary to Represent Data about Traffic supports in-situ and remote observations, but not models. Nevertheless, a snapshot of traffic in a city can be obtained if it is used in conjunction with vocabularies to represent city road maps. In [16], sensors can be located into vehicles or as part of an infrastructure element of the roads, but remote sensing is not considered. Besides, a road agent can provide information on the road in only three particular cases: short-term, long-term, or anticipatory; but does not support dynamic traffic models. open511 and Road Accident Ontology provide information about road events (traffic or road accidents in Road Accident Ontology) that can be considered observable properties or features of interest of road sections but do not support either traffic models or data models for sensing.

TAQE fulfills all the requirements. Regarding traffic data, it supports in-situ data only partially since only fixed stations are supported. Remote sensing devices and other observation mechanisms that support the observation of various locations at the same time are not supported yet.

7   Conclusions

This paper presented a data modeling framework, called TAQE, for the representation of observation and modeled data in the air quality and traffic application domains. The model is integrated into level 3 of the information architecture of four levels of abstraction, which is based on the extensive use of reputed international standards. Both TAQE and all the other models found in the literature for air quality and traffic data were evaluated concerning a collection of requirements extracted from a comprehensive set of applications. Besides, the application of TAQE to a real use case in the scope of the TRAFAIR EU project was also undertaken, showing the utility of the model and its potential to both reduce development costs and to ease semantic data integration between different areas in the same application domain, but also between different application domains, enabling this way the implementation of tools of a more general purpose. Future work is related to the extension of the traffic model to support removable in-situ devices and remote sensing.

Acknowledgement. This research was supported by the TRAFAIR project (2017-EU-IA-0167), co-financed by the Connecting Europe Facility of the European Union, and by the NEAT-Ambience project (Next-gEnerATion dAta Management to foster suitable Behaviors and the resilience of cItizens against modErN ChallEnges PID2020-113037RB-I00 / AEI / 10.13039/501100011033). We thank reviewers who provided insight to improve the final version of this paper.

References

1. Bachechi, C., Desimoni, F., Po, L., Casas, D.M.: Visual analytics for spatio-temporal air quality data. In: 24th International Conference on Information Visualisation, IV 2020, Melbourne, Australia, 7–11 September 2020, pp. 460–466. IEEE (2020)
2. Bachechi, C., Po, L.: Implementing an urban dynamic traffic model. In: Barnaghi, P.M., Gottlob, G., Manolopoulos, Y., Tzouramanis, T., Vakali, A. (eds.) 2019 IEEE/WIC/ACM International Conference on Web Intelligence, WI 2019, Thessaloniki, Greece, 14–17 October 2019, pp. 312–316. ACM (2019)
3. Bachechi, C., Po, L.: Traffic analysis in a smart city. In: Proceedings - 2019 IEEE/WIC/ACM International Conference on Web Intelligence Workshops, WI 2019 Companion, pp. 275–282. Association for Computing Machinery Inc. (2019)
4. Bachechi, C., Po, L., Rollo, F.: Big data analytics and visualization in traffic monitoring. Big Data Res. **27**, 100292 (2022)
5. Bachechi, C., Rollo, F., Desimoni, F., Po, L.: Using real sensors data to calibrate a traffic model for the city of Modena. Adv. Intell. Syst. Comput. **1131**(AISC), 468–473 (2020)
6. Bachechi, C., Rollo, F., Po, L.: Real-time data cleaning in traffic sensor networks. In: 17th IEEE/ACS International Conference on Computer Systems and Applications, AICCSA 2020, Antalya, Turkey, 2–5 November 2020, pp. 1–8. IEEE (2020)
7. Bachechi, C., Rollo, F., Po, L.: Detection and classification of sensor anomalies for simulating urban traffic scenarios. Cluster Comput., 1–25 (2021). https://doi.org/10.1007/s10586-021-03445-7
8. Bigi, A., Veratti, G., Fabbi, S., Po, L., Ghermandi, G.: Forecast of the impact by local emissions at an urban micro scale by the combination of Lagrangian modelling and low cost sensing technology: the TRAFAIR project. In: 19th International Conference on Harmonisation within Atmospheric Dispersion Modelling for Regulatory Purposes, Harmo 2019 (2019)
9. Bizer, C., Heath, T., Berners-Lee, T.: Linked data - the story so far. Int. J. Semant. Web Inf. Syst. **5**(3), 1–22 (2009)
10. Compton, M., et al.: The SSN ontology of the W3C semantic sensor network incubator group. Web Semant. Sci. Serv. Agents World Wide Web **17**, 25–32 (2012)
11. Cox, S.: ISO 19156:2011 - Geographic Information - Observations and Measurements. International Organization for Standardization, January 2011
12. Desimoni, F., Ilarri, S., Po, L., Rollo, F., Trillo-Lado, R.: Semantic traffic sensor data: the TRAFAIR experience. Appl. Sci. (Switzerland) **10**(17), 5882 (2020)
13. Djahel, S., Doolan, R., Muntean, G.-M., Murphy, J.: A communications-oriented perspective on traffic management systems for smart cities: challenges & innovative approaches. IEEE Commun. Surv. Tutorials **17**(1), 125–151 (2015)
14. Dombalyan, A., Kocherga, V., Semchugova, E., Negrov, N.: Traffic forecasting model for a road section. Transp. Res. Procedia **20**, 159–165. 12th International Conference on Organization and Traffic Safety Management in large cities, SPbOTSIC-2016, 28–30 September 2016, St. Petersburg, Russia (2017)

15. Elloumi, M., Dhaou, R., Escrig, B., Idoudi, H., Saidane, L.A.: Monitoring road traffic with a UAV-based system. In: 2018 IEEE Wireless Communications and Networking Conference (WCNC), pp. 1–6 (2018)
16. Fernandez, S., Hadfi, R., Ito, T., Marsa-Maestre, I., Velasco, J.: Ontology-based architecture for intelligent transportation systems using a traffic sensor network. Sensors 16(8), 1287 (2016)
17. Galárraga, L., Mathiassen, K.A.M., Hose, K.: QBOAirbase: the European air quality database as an RDF cube. In: International Semantic Web Conference (2017)
18. Gomez-Perez, A., Fernández-López, M., Corcho, O.: Ontological Engineering: with Examples from the Areas of Knowledge Management, E-Commerce and the Semantic Web. Springer, London, January 2004. https://doi.org/10.1007/b97353
19. Hou, Y., Edara, P., Sun, C.: Traffic flow forecasting for urban work zones. IEEE Trans. Intell. Transp. Syst. 16(4), 1761–1770 (2015)
20. Ilarri, S., Wolfson, O., Delot, T.: Collaborative sensing for urban transportation. IEEE Data Eng. Bull. 37(4), 3–14 (2014)
21. Janowicz, K., Haller, A., Cox, S.J., Phuoc, D.L., Lefrançois, M.: SOSA: a lightweight ontology for sensors, observations, samples, and actuators. J. Web Seman. 56, 1–10 (2019)
22. Kaivonen, S., Ngai, E.C.-H.: Real-time air pollution monitoring with sensors on city bus. Digit. Commun. Netw. 6(1), 23–30 (2020)
23. Martin, R.V.: Satellite remote sensing of surface air quality. Atmos. Environ. 42(34), 7823–7843 (2008)
24. Martín, J., Khatib, E.J., Lázaro, P., Barco, R.: Traffic monitoring via mobile device location. Sensors 19(20), 4505 (2019)
25. Métral, C., Falquet, G., Karatzas, K.D.: Ontologies for the integration of air quality models and 3D city models. ArXiv, abs/1201.6511 (2012)
26. Nesi, P., Po, L., Viqueira, J.R.R., Trillo-Lado, R.: An integrated smart city platform. In: Szymański, J., Velegrakis, Y. (eds.) IKC 2017. LNCS, vol. 10546, pp. 171–176. Springer, Cham (2018). https://doi.org/10.1007/978-3-319-74497-1_17
27. Oprea, M.M.: Air_POLLUTION_ONTO: an ontology for air pollution analysis and control. In: Iliadis, M., Tsoumakasis, V., Bramer (eds.) Artificial Intelligence Applications and Innovations III, pp. 135–143. Springer, Boston (2009). https://doi.org/10.1007/978-1-4419-0221-4_17
28. Po, L., Rollo, F., Bachechi, C., Corni, A.: From sensors data to urban traffic flow analysis. In: 2019 IEEE International Smart Cities Conference, ISC2 2019, Casablanca, Morocco, 14–17 October 2019, pp. 478–485. IEEE (2019)
29. Po, L., et al.: TRAFAIR: understanding traffic flow to improve air quality. In: 2019 IEEE International Smart Cities Conference, ISC2, pp. 36–43 (2019)
30. Regueiro, M.A., Viqueira, J.R., Stasch, C., Taboada, J.A.: Semantic mediation of observation datasets through sensor observation services. Future Gener. Comput. Syst. 67, 47–56 (2017)
31. Regueiro, M.A., Viqueira, J.R., Taboada, J.A., Cotos, J.M.: Virtual integration of sensor observation data. Comput. Geosci. 81, 12–19 (2015)
32. Riga, M., Moumtzidou, A., Vrochidis, S., Kompatsiaris, I., Syropoulou, P.: D4.2: semantic integration and reasoning of environmental data. Technical report, CERTH (2017)
33. Rohi, G., Ejofodomi, O., Ofualagba, G.: Autonomous monitoring, analysis, and countering of air pollution using environmental drones. Heliyon 6, e03252 (2020)
34. Rollo, F., Po, L.: SenseBoard: sensor monitoring for air quality experts. In: Costa, C., Pitoura, E. (eds.) Proceedings of the Workshops of the EDBT/ICDT 2021

Joint Conference, Nicosia, Cyprus, 23 March 2021, vol. 2841. CEUR Workshop Proceedings. CEUR-WS.org (2021)

35. Rollo, F., Sudharsan, B., Po, L., Breslin, J.G.: Air quality sensor network data acquisition, cleaning, visualization, and analytics: a real-world IoT use case. In: Doryab, A., Lv, Q., Beigl, M. (eds.) UbiComp/ISWC 2021: 2021 ACM International Joint Conference on Pervasive and Ubiquitous Computing and 2021 ACM International Symposium on Wearable Computers, Virtual Event, 21–25 September 2021, pp. 67–68. ACM (2021)

36. Sharif, A., Li, J., Khalil, M., Kumar, R., Sharif, M.I., Sharif, A.: Internet of things—smart traffic management system for smart cities using big data analytics. In: 14th International Computer Conference on Wavelet Active Media Technology and Information Processing (ICCWAMTIP 2017). IEEE, December 2017

Using Graphs to Represent Japanese Words for Serious Games

Tristan Tribes[1], Virgil Rouquette-Campredon[1], Samuel Helye[1],
and Madalina Croitoru[2]([✉])

[1] Computer Science Department, Faculty of Science, University of Montpellier,
Montpellier, France
[2] Boreal, LIRMM, INRIA, CNRS, University of Montpellier, Montpellier, France
croitoru@lirmm.fr

Abstract. The aim of this paper is to explore the representation problem of how Japanese words are constructed from Kanjis (i.e. symbols for concepts). We discuss the various implications of such representations and demonstrate a fully functional game built upon a Neo4J implementation.

1 Introduction

The main contribution of this paper is to discuss the graph based knowledge representation and reasoning aspects behind the implementation of a serious online Japanese learning game: Lost My Pieces. Graph based knowledge representation and reasoning techniques have been historically investigated in the International Conference on Conceptual Structures (ICCS) community [10]. Starting with work on Conceptual Graphs [2,14], Concept Graphs [5], Existential Graphs [8] or, more recently, Argumentation Graphs [6] the main idea behind such graph representations is simple. Using a graph based representation of the problem and by translating the reasoning task, in a sound and complete manner, into a graph operation, one can benefit from combinatorial optimisations from the graph theoretical world for practical reasoning task [3]. For example, by having positive existentially closed deduction of logical formulae translated into labelled graph homomorphism, one can unveil query structures that yield excellent results in practice [4].

In this paper we place ourselves in the context of graph based knowledge representation and reasoning and answer the following research questions: "How to represent kanji combination for facilitating the learning of the Japanese language?". In order to endorse the feasibility of the solution we also demonstrate a fully functional serious game [1,7,11,13,15] that allows users to learn Japanese online and discuss various paths for future developments.

2 Motivating Example

Imagine a student that is keen to learn Japanese. The Japanese language, notoriously difficult, is composed of three writing systems. The most difficult one is

called kanji, where each ideogram represent a concept or an idea, and can be
by itself a whole word. There are about 2000 kanjis to learn in order to be able
to simply carry on a day to day task such as reading a newspaper. To further
the difficulty of the learning, combining kanjis can give birth to new words. For
instance combining the kanji for woman (女) with the kanji for day (日) gives
the word Sun goddess (日女). Similarly, the kanji for one (一) together with
the kanji for person (人) gives the word alone (一人).

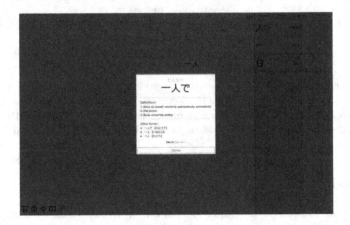

Fig. 1. Screenshot of lost my pieces

Despite its beauty, it is complicated to keep motivation up when learning
Japanese. To counter this problem we propose a novel way of learning by means
of an interactive platform. The intuition of the interaction is inspired by the
game Little Alchemy[1] [9] that allows the combination of pictograms in order to
make new images.

In our platform, called Lost My Pieces[2], the user is presented with a set of
basic kanjis. The user can drag and drop the kanjis onto the central pane (called
whiteboard) and combine them to discover new words. In Fig. 1 a screenshot of
the combination of the two kanjis person and one is depicted. Please notice three
important aspects:

- First, albeit impossible to render on a picture, the stroke order required for
  writing the kanji is also depicted when the kanji is selected, facilitating the
  learning of writing.
- Second, in an attempt to render the platform pleasant to use we established
  a point system allowing the user to unlock kanjis according to their budget.
  This is visible in Fig. 2 that shows all possible kanjis to unlock (and thus to
  further combine).

[1] https://littlealchemy.com/.
[2] https://lostmypieces.com/.

– Third, when searching for a new kanji to unlock, one can directly see how many new words they will be able to create with this newly acquired kanji using their already existing ones. However, such functionality will render the representation task more difficult as explained in Sect. 3.

In order to code the platform we have used a common client-server architecture. On the client side we have used the JavaScript library React. On the server side we have used Node.js®, a Javascript run-time environment and the Fastify framework. For storing data we have used Neo4j. In the following section we will detail the implementation solution. Then, in Sect. 3 we will explain the data storage problem and our contribution.

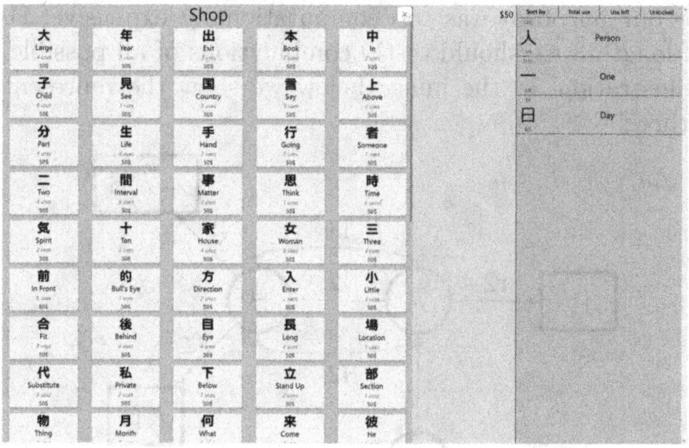

Fig. 2. Screenshot of lost my pieces shop

The technologies used for developing the platform as follows:

– React (front end): Allows for faster UI development, with reusable components and seamless page update and interactions.
– Fastify (back end, REST API): Fast API framework to serve database requests to the end-user.
– NodeJS (back end): Javascript run-time to handle all server related tasks.
– NGINX (server): Handles all traffic towards the server.

We have purposely not described the Neo4j component as knowledge representation and reasoning issues are detailed in the next section.

3   Representation Problems

The representation problem we address in this paper is the following. We consider a list of kanjis $\mathcal{K}$. For each kanji $k \in \mathcal{K}$ I need to store the meaning of the kanji and, for elements of $\mathcal{K} \setminus \{k\}$ their combined meaning. For example, we can consider A and B two kanjis. The word AB respects the order of its components (i.e. A is first, B is second) and its meaning is different from BA. To represent this using a database we explored several possibilities.

First we considered using a graph where the nodes could either be kanjis or words and the edges are labelled using the length of the corresponding word. We exploit paths as follows:

While using this method we could exploit paths (i.e. represent words) of arbitrary length. Unfortunately, the main problem is that manipulating this structure (for our purpose) was too computationally expensive. For example, for a word of length 3 we should test 9 combinations of all possible orders (i.e. paths). For illustration, in the image below we show the representation for a word of size three.

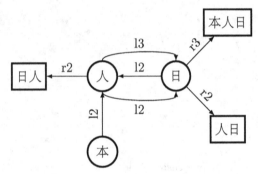

A second solution consisted of labelling the edges in the graph as words (with nodes only representing kanjis). This solution is depicted below.

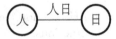

The advantage of this representation is that we can represent all orders by simply checking if an edge label exists.

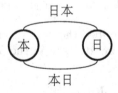

However, the words of length 3 or more require a hypergraph support. Furthermore, it requires to have self cycles (for words that contain repeating kanjis). The hypergraph depiction is shown below.

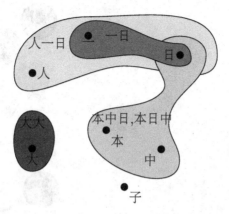

The main problem with the hypergraph representation was the fact that a word could have several definitions and different variations. For example the word obtained by combining the kanji large and book has two definitions: root and foundation. Furthermore it has two different reading possibilities depending on the context. If this word is represented as an hyperedge we will need further combinatorial elements to add the information above.

Our solution it to represent the hypergraph as a bipartite graph as follows.

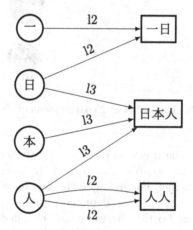

In this final solution (the one that we decided to implement using Neo4j) the bipartite graph [12, 16] contains two classes of nodes. On one hand the kanjis (represented as round nodes, on the left) and, on the other hand, the words, represented as rectangles, on the right part of the graph. The edges are labelled with the length of the word they lead to. This allows for querying, by kanji, the words of a given length. The different forms or definitions of a word could be represented as attributes on the words, or additional nodes connected to their associated words.

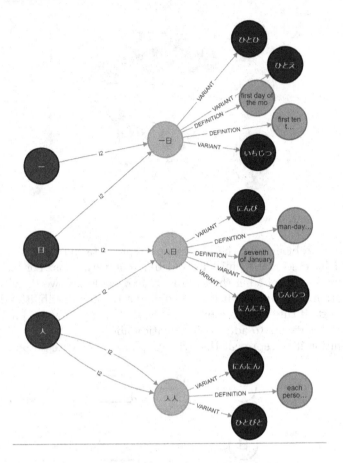

Fig. 3. Screenshot of Neo4j implementation

This combinatorial structure is implemented in Neo4j. In Fig. 3, in orange we depict three kanjis for day, one and person. In blue we depict the words constructed with these kanjis. For instance the top most blue node represents men day with three different readings depicted in red.

Overall, in our platform LostMyPieces we have encoded the 101 most frequent kanjis resulting in a JSON file of size 1 545 KB. With these kanjis we can make 2711 words. The size of the resulting graph is of 10436 nodes and 6563 edges (as follows l2 : 3618 / l3 : 2064 / l4 : 756 / l5 : 125).

To read a newspaper we should consider 2136 kanjis (that are taught at school and allow to form 100694 words). We encoded this in Neo4J resulting in a JSON file of size: 51 813 KB. The resulting graph consists of 319 591 nodes and 295

095 edges, with words made of up to 18 kanjis[3]. Both graphs are available upon request.

4   Evaluation and Discussion

In this paper we have demonstrated how using a graph based knowledge representation solution can be practically used in the context of a serious game allowing users to learn Japanese. For far our evaluation has been purely functionality oriented. We have held several game sessions with various level users that have then returned an evaluation sheet deeming themselves satisfied by our game. Ideally we would like to test our game with two classes of users, having similar Japanese language skills. They will carry on learning the language over a period of time and then we could assess the effectiveness of the plateform. Such effort is, for now, impossible to put in practice. However we are quite optimistic with respect to the effectiveness of our game because it allows the user to understand how the construction of the word takes place (as opposed to just simply memorising it). We thus hypothesise that such approach will yield better learning results.

Several future work directions are currently considered. First, several questions regarding the development of the game could be considered. Can we add more information on words? How they are linked, do they have similar structure? Can we use N5 to N1 Japanese levels to categorise our words? Can we create new imaginary words from this whole database? Instead of using all Japanese words, could we instead use a list of important words from Japanese learning methods? Can we use the shop to see what people would usually buy first? Can we randomise the shop to alleviate the order bias (buying the first one, or buying the one with most uses)?

From a representation point of view, the Neo4j database is not local and having delays on every requests is painful. Can we develop our own local solution for graph database that works inside browser? How suitable is an RDF representation of the structure and could RDF/S rules bring new information relevant to the game?

Acknowledgement. The authors acknowledge the participants of Imagine Master class at University of Montpellier for the provided user data. We also thank M. Lafourcade for his feedback and giving us the opportunity to work together.

References

1. Abt, C.C.: Serious Games. University Press of America, Lanham (1987)
2. Chein, M., Mugnier, M.-L.: Graph-based Knowledge Representation: Computational Foundations Of Conceptual Graphs. Springer, London (2008). https://doi.org/10.1007/978-1-84800-286-9

---

[3] 公共土木施設災害復旧事業費国庫負担法 : National Government Defrayment Act for Reconstruction of Disaster-Stricken Public Facilities.

3. Chein, M., Mugnier, M.-L., Croitoru, M.: Visual reasoning with graph-based mechanisms: the good, the better and the best. Knowl. Eng. Rev. **28**(3), 249–271 (2013)
4. Croitoru, M., Compatangelo, E.: A tree decomposition algorithm for conceptual graph projection. In: KR, pp. 271–276 (2006)
5. Dau, F.: Concept graphs and predicate logic. In: Delugach, H.S., Stumme, G. (eds.) ICCS-ConceptStruct 2001. LNCS (LNAI), vol. 2120, pp. 72–86. Springer, Heidelberg (2001). https://doi.org/10.1007/3-540-44583-8_6
6. Dung, P.M.: An argumentation-theoretic foundation for logic programming. J. Logic Program. **22**(2), 151–177 (1995)
7. Johnson, W.L., Vilhjálmsson, H.H., Marsella, S.: Serious games for language learning: how much game, how much AI?. In: AIED, vol. 125, pp. 306–313 (2005)
8. Ketner, K.L.: Pierce's existential graphs as the basis for an introduction to logic: Semiosis in the logic classroom. In: Semiotics 1980, pp. 231–239. Springer, Boston (1982). https://doi.org/10.1007/978-1-4684-9137-1_23
9. Leino, O.T.: Stone+ life= egg-little alchemy as a limit-idea for thinking about knowledge and discovery in computer games. In: Proceedings of Philosophy of Computer Games Conference (2016)
10. Mineau, G.W., Moulin, B., Sowa, J.F. (eds.): ICCS-ConceptStruct 1993. LNCS, vol. 699. Springer, Heidelberg (1993). https://doi.org/10.1007/3-540-56979-0
11. Ritterfeld, U., Cody, M., Vorderer, P.: Serious Games: Mechanisms and Effects. Routledge, London (2009)
12. Serratosa, F.: Fast computation of bipartite graph matching. Pattern Recogn. Lett. **45**, 244–250 (2014)
13. Sørensen, B.H., Meyer, B.: Serious games in language learning and teaching-a theoretical perspective. In: DiGRA Conference, pp. 559–566 (2007)
14. Sowa, J.F.: Conceptual graphs for a data base interface. IBM J. Res. Dev. **20**(4), 336–357 (1976)
15. Susi, T., Johannesson, M., Backlund, P.: Serious games: an overview (2007)
16. Zha, H., He, X., Ding, C., Simon, H., Gu, M.: Bipartite graph partitioning and data clustering. In: Proceedings of the Tenth International Conference on Information and Knowledge Management, pp. 25–32 (2001)

Lattices and Formal Concept Analyses

Attribute Exploration with Multiple Contradicting Partial Experts

Maximilian Felde[1,2]([⊠]) [iD] and Gerd Stumme[1,2] [iD]

[1] Knowledge and Data Engineering Group, University of Kassel, Kassel, Germany
[2] Interdisciplinary Research Center for Information System Design,
University of Kassel, Kassel, Germany
{felde,stumme}@cs.uni-kassel.de

Abstract. Attribute exploration is a method from Formal Concept Analysis (FCA) that helps a domain expert discover structural dependencies in knowledge domains which can be represented as formal contexts (cross tables of objects and attributes). In this paper we present an extension of attribute exploration that allows for a group of domain experts and explores their shared views. Each expert has their own view of the domain and the views of multiple experts may contain contradicting information.

Keywords: Formal concept analysis · Attribute exploration ·
Incomplete information · Multiple experts

1 Introduction

Attribute exploration [7] is a well known knowledge acquisition method from Formal Concept Analysis (FCA) [11]. In domains that can be represented as formal contexts (binary tables that capture the relation between objects and attributes), attribute exploration allows a domain expert to efficiently discover all attribute dependencies in the domain.

The basic idea of attribute exploration is to extend domain information using a question-answering scheme with answers provided by a domain expert. The questions are posed in the form of implications over the attributes of the domain. The attribute exploration algorithm determines the next question $A_1 \ldots A_n \to B$? (read: Do attributes $A_1 \ldots A_n$ imply attribute B in the domain?) which the expert then either confirms or refutes. If the expert refutes the implication then a counterexample has to be provided, i.e., an object from the domain that has the attributes $A_1 \ldots A_n$ but lacks attribute B. The algorithm poses these questions until the validity of every conceivable implication can be inferred from the obtained domain information, i.e., every implication either follows from the accepted implications or one of the examples serves as counterexample.

In the basic setting, attribute exploration requires a single all-knowing expert. Extensions that allow for background information [8,19] and for an expert with partial knowledge [3,15–17] have been developed. However, these are just two

T. Braun et al. (Eds.): ICCS 2022, LNCS 13403, pp. 51–65, 2022.
https://doi.org/10.1007/978-3-031-16663-1_5

examples from a vast body of extensions and variations that have been studied. An extensive overview can be found in the book *Conceptual Exploration* [10].

Despite the many advances to attribute exploration, its extension to multiple experts has only recently gained interest, cf. [4,5,14,18]. And, except for [5], the basic assumption made is that some true universe exists (for a given domain).

In this paper we generalize the approach of [5] and suggest a framework for attribute exploration with multiple experts without the assumption of the existence of some true universe. Here, multiple experts can have contradicting views of a domain. Contradicting views occur naturally in domains that are subjective (e.g. opinions). Our approach also allows for the situations where some true universe exists but the experts may be imperfect and make mistakes when answering questions. Our aim is to identify both the common and the conflicting views. The resolution of those conflicts is out of the scope of our approach.

The paper is structured as follows: In Sect. 2, we recollect the basics of FCA and how to model incomplete information in FCA via incomplete contexts, possible and certain derivations, information order and satisfiable implications. In the main section, Sect. 3, we first discuss the problem of attribute exploration with multiple experts. Then, we introduce a representation of expert views of a domain and the notion of shared implications. We provide an algorithm to explore the shared implication theory for a group of experts and discuss how to explore the shared implication theories for some or all subsets of a group of experts. Afterwards, we discuss how this approach can be used as a first step in a collaborative exploration to find a common view and identify the conflicts that exist among the group of experts. Finally, we provide conclusion and outlook in Sect. 4. In order to keep the paper as concise as possible we provide an example only in the arXiv version[1]. Note that we do not provide a separate section for related work and instead combine it with the recollection of the basics and provide context on related work where appropriate.

2   Foundations

FCA was introduced by Wille in [20]. As the theory matured, Ganter and Wille compiled the mathematical foundations of the theory in [11]. We begin by recalling some notions from FCA and some extensions that allow us to model incomplete and conditional information.

2.1   Formal Concept Analysis

Formal Context and Concept. A *formal context* $\mathbb{K} = (G, M, I)$ consists of a set G of objects, a set M of attributes and an incidence relation $I \subseteq G \times M$ with $(g, m) \in I$ meaning "*object g has attribute m*". There are several interpretations for $(g, m) \notin I$, cf. [2,3], the standard one being, "*g does not have the attribute m or it is irrelevant, whether g has m*". In the following we interpret $(g, m) \notin I$ as "*g does not have m*", which is reasonable when modeling incomplete knowledge.

---

[1] https://doi.org/10.48550/arXiv.2205.15714.

This interpretation can be equivalently modeled by a (two-valued) *formal context* $\mathbb{K} = (G, M, I)$ that consists of a set of objects G, a set of attributes M and an *incidence function* $I\colon G \times M \to \{\times, o\}$. The incidence function describes whether an object g has an attribute m: $I(g, m) = \times$ means "*g has m*" and $I(g, m) = o$ means "*g does not have m*".[2] Clearly we can use a one-valued formal context to define an equivalent two-valued formal context and vice versa using $(g, m) \in I \Leftrightarrow I(g, m) = \times$. In the following we will use these two notations interchangeably. Two derivation operators $(\cdot)'\colon \mathcal{P}(M) \to \mathcal{P}(G)$ and $(\cdot)'\colon \mathcal{P}(G) \to \mathcal{P}(M)$ are defined in the following way: For a set of objects $A \subseteq G$, the set of *attributes common to the objects in A* is provided by $A' := \{m \in M \mid \forall g \in A : (g, m) \in I\}$. Analogously, for a set of attributes $B \subseteq M$, the set of *objects that have all the attributes from B* is provided by $B' := \{g \in G \mid \forall m \in B : (g, m) \in I\}$. To prevent ambiguity if we have multiple contexts, we use the incidence relation I and write A^I instead of A'. For a single object $g \in G$ (or attribute) we omit the parentheses and simply write g'. A *formal concept* of a formal context $\mathbb{K} = (G, M, I)$ is a pair (A, B) with $A \subseteq G$ and $B \subseteq M$ such that $A' = B$ and $A = B'$. A is called the *extent* and B the *intent* of the formal concept (A, B). The set of all formal concepts of a context $\mathbb{K}$ is denoted by $\mathfrak{B}(\mathbb{K})$. Note that for any set $A \subseteq G$ the set A' is the intent of a concept and for any set $B \subseteq M$ the set B' is the extent of a concept. The subconcept-superconcept relation on $\mathfrak{B}(\mathbb{K})$ is formalized by: $(A_1, B_1) \leq (A_2, B_2) :\Leftrightarrow A_1 \subseteq A_2 (\Leftrightarrow B_1 \supseteq B_2)$. The set of concepts together with this order relation $(\mathfrak{B}(\mathbb{K}), \leq)$, also denoted $\mathfrak{B}(\mathbb{K})$, forms a complete lattice, the *concept lattice*. The vertical combination of two formal contexts $\mathbb{K}_i = (G_i, M, I_i), i \in \{1, 2\}$ on the same set of attributes M is called the *subposition* of $\mathbb{K}_1$ and $\mathbb{K}_2$ which is denoted by $\frac{\mathbb{K}_1}{\mathbb{K}_2}$. Formally, it is defined as $(\dot{G}_1 \cup \dot{G}_2, M, \dot{I}_1 \cup \dot{I}_2)$, where $\dot{G}_i := \{i\} \times G$ and $\dot{I}_i := \{((i, g), m) \mid (g, m) \in I_i\}$ for $i \in \{1, 2\}$. The *subposition* of a set of contexts $\{\mathbb{K}_1, \ldots, \mathbb{K}_n\}$ on the same set of attributes is defined analogously and we denote this by $\dot{\div}_{i \in \{1, \ldots, n\}} \mathbb{K}_i$.

Attribute Implications. Let M be a finite set of attributes. An *attribute implication* over M is a pair of subsets $A, B \subseteq M$, denoted by $A \to B$, cf. [11]. A is called the *premise* and B the *conclusion* of the implication $A \to B$. The set of all implications over a set M is denoted by $\text{Imp}_M = \{A \to B \mid A, B \subseteq M\}$.

A subset $T \subseteq M$ *respects* an attribute implication $A \to B$ over M if $A \not\subseteq T$ or $B \subseteq T$. Such a set T is also called a *model* of the implication. T *respects a set $\mathcal{L}$ of implications* if T respects all implications in $\mathcal{L}$. An implication $A \to B$ *holds* in a set of subsets of M if each of these subsets respects the implication. Mod $\mathcal{L}$ denotes the set of all attribute sets that respect a set of implications $\mathcal{L}$; it is a closure system on M. The respective closure operator is denoted with $\mathcal{L}(\cdot)$.

For a formal context $\mathbb{K} = (G, M, I)$ an implication $A \to B$ over M *holds in the context* if for every object $g \in G$ the object intent g' respects the implication. Such an implication $A \to B$ is also called a *valid implication* of $\mathbb{K}$. Further, an implication $A \to B$ holds in $\mathbb{K}$ if and only if $B \subseteq A''$, or equivalently $A' \subseteq B'$.

---

[2] For modeling incomplete information, we later extend $\{\times, o\}$ by "?", cf. Definition 2.1.

The set of all implications that hold in a formal context $\mathbb{K}$ is denoted by $\mathrm{Imp}(\mathbb{K})$. An implication $A \to B$ *follows* from a set $\mathcal{L}$ of implications over M if each subset of M respecting $\mathcal{L}$ also respects $A \to B$. A family of implications is called *closed* if every implication following from $\mathcal{L}$ is already contained in $\mathcal{L}$. Closed sets of implications are also called *implication theories*. For an implication theory $\mathcal{L}$ on M, the context $\mathbb{K} = (\mathrm{Mod}\ \mathcal{L}, M, \ni)$ is a context such that $\mathrm{Imp}(\mathbb{K}) = \mathcal{L}$ and $\mathcal{L}$ is the system of all concept intents. Because the number of implications that hold in some context $\mathbb{K}$ can be very large, one usually works with a subset $\mathcal{L}$ of implications that is *sound* (implications in $\mathcal{L}$ hold in $\mathbb{K}$), *complete* (implications that hold in $\mathbb{K}$ follow from $\mathcal{L}$) and *irredundant* (no implication in $\mathcal{L}$ follows from other implications in $\mathcal{L}$). Such a subset of implications is also called *implication base*. A specific base with minimal size is the so-called *canonical base*, cf. [11,13].

Attribute Exploration. Attribute exploration is a method to uncover the implication theory for a domain with the help of a domain expert. It works by asking the expert questions about the validity of implications in the domain. The basic approach [7] computes the canonical base. This requires the expert to have a complete view of the domain and respond to a question *does $R \to S$ hold?* by either confirming that the implication holds in the domain or by rejecting that it holds with a counterexample, i.e., an object g from the domain together with all its relations to the attributes such that $R \subseteq g'$ but $S \not\subseteq g'$. The exploration algorithm successively poses questions until all implications can either be inferred to follow from the set of accepted implications or be rejected based on some counterexample. More precisely, the questions are usually asked in lectic order with respect to the premise R (which can be computed with the *NextClosure* algorithm, c.f. [7,10,11]) and the conclusion S is the largest set of attributes that can follow from R with respect to the examples provided so far.

Many extensions and variants of attribute exploration have been developed since its introduction in [7]. Some examples are the use of background information and exceptions studied by Stumme [19] and Ganter [8] and the use of incomplete information studied by Holzer and Burmeister [2,3,15–17]. A good overview can be found in *Conceptual Exploration* [10] by Ganter and Obiedkov.

Relative Canonical Base. The canonical base has been generalized to allow for (background) implications [19] as prior information. We use this extensively in Sect. 3.1 when we explore all shared implications for a group of experts.

Assuming we have a formal context $\mathbb{K} = (G, M, I)$ and a set of (background) implications $\mathcal{L}_0$ on M that hold in the context $\mathbb{K}$, a *pseudo-intent* of $\mathbb{K}$ *relative to $\mathcal{L}_0$*, or *$\mathcal{L}_0$-pseudo-intent*, is a set $P \subseteq M$ with the properties:

1. P respects $\mathcal{L}_0$
2. $P \neq P''$
3. If $Q \subseteq P$, $Q \neq P$, is an $\mathcal{L}_0$-pseudo-intent of $\mathbb{K}$ then $Q'' \subseteq P$.

The set $\mathcal{L}_{\mathbb{K}\mathcal{L}_0} := \{P \to P'' | P$ an $\mathcal{L}_0$-pseudo-intent of $\mathbb{K}\}$ is called the *canonical base* of $\mathbb{K}$ *relative to $\mathcal{L}_0$*, or simply the *relative canonical base*. Note that all implications in $\mathcal{L}_{\mathbb{K}\mathcal{L}_0}$ hold in $\mathbb{K}$. Further (see [9,19]), if all implications of $\mathcal{L}_0$ hold in $\mathbb{K}$, then

1. each implication that holds in $\mathbb{K}$ follows from $\mathcal{L}_{\mathbb{K}\mathcal{L}_0} \cup \mathcal{L}_0$, and
2. $\mathcal{L}_{\mathbb{K}\mathcal{L}_0}$ is irredundant w.r.t. 1.

2.2 Incomplete Information in FCA

In order to model partial information about a domain we use the notion of an *incomplete context*, a special multi-valued context, which can be interpreted as a formal context with some missing information. This notion of partial information has been extensively studied by Burmeister and Holzer, c.f. [3,15–17]. We now recollect some notions.

Incomplete Context

Definition 2.1. *An* incomplete context *is defined as a three-valued context* $\mathbb{K} = (G, M, W, I)$ *consisting of a set of objects* G, *a set of attributes* M, *a set of values* $W = \{\times, o, ?\}$ *and an incidence function* $I\colon G \times M \to \{\times, o, ?\}$. *For* $g \in G$ *and* $m \in M$ *we say that* "g has m" *if* $I(g, m) = \times$, "g does not have m" *if* $I(g, m) = o$ *and* "it is not known whether g has m" *if* $I(g, m) =?$.

Another possibility to model incomplete information about the relation between objects and attributes is to use a pair of formal contexts $(\mathbb{K}_+, \mathbb{K}_?)$ on the same sets of objects and attributes such that $\mathbb{K}_+$ models the attributes that the objects certainly have and $\mathbb{K}_?$ models the attributes that the objects might have, c.f. [8,10]. This is equivalent to our representation as incomplete context.

The subposition for incomplete contexts $\mathbb{K}_i = (G_i, M, W, I_i), i \in \{1, 2\}$ is the incomplete context $\frac{\mathbb{K}_1}{\mathbb{K}_2} = (\dot{G}_1 \cup \dot{G}_2, M, W, I)$ where $I((i, g), m) = I_i(g, m)$. The *subposition* of a set of incomplete contexts $\{\mathbb{K}_1, \ldots, \mathbb{K}_n\}$ on the same set of attributes is defined analogously and denoted by $\dot{\leftthreetimes}_{i \in \{1, \ldots, n\}} \mathbb{K}_i$.

Information Order. On the values $\{\times, o, ?\}$ of incomplete contexts we define the *information order* $\leq$ where $? \leq \times$, $? \leq o$ and $\times$ and o are incomparable, c.f. [1,6,12,15]. This order is used to compare different incomplete contexts on the same set of attributes in the following way: Given two incomplete contexts $\mathbb{K}_1 = (G_1, M, W, I_1)$ and $\mathbb{K}_2 = (G_2, M, W, I_2)$ we say that $\mathbb{K}_2$ contains at least as much information as $\mathbb{K}_1$, denoted $\mathbb{K}_1 \leq \mathbb{K}_2$ if $G_1 \subseteq G_2$ and for all $(g, m) \in G_1 \times M$ we have $I_1(g, m) \leq I_2(g, m)$ in the information order.

For two incomplete contexts $\mathbb{K}_1$ and $\mathbb{K}_2$ on the same set of attributes M that have no conflicting information, i.e., when there is no $g \in G_1 \cap G_2$, $m \in M$ with $I_1(g, m)$ and $I_2(g, m)$ incomparable, their supremum $\mathbb{K}_1 \vee \mathbb{K}_2 := (G_1 \cup G_2, M, W, I)$ is obtained by defining $I(g, m)$ as supremum of $I_1(g, m)$ and $I_2(g, m)$ where $I_i(g, m) := ?$ if $g \notin G_i$.

Incomplete contexts that contain no "?" are identified with the respective formal context. A *completion* of an incomplete context $\mathbb{K}$ is a formal context $\hat{\mathbb{K}}$ with $\mathbb{K} \leq \hat{\mathbb{K}}$.

Derivation Operators for Incomplete Contexts. The derivation operator $\cdot'$ is only defined for formal contexts, however, there are some analogue operators for incomplete contexts that capture the notions of possible and certain relations.

Given an incomplete context $\mathbb{K} = (G, M, W, I)$ the *certain intent* for $A \subseteq G$ is defined by $A^\square := \{m \in M \mid I(g, m) = \times \text{ for all } g \in A\}$ and the *possible intent* by $A^\Diamond := \{m \in M \mid I(g, m) \neq o \text{ for all } g \in A\}$. For $B \subseteq M$ the *certain extent* $B^\square$ and the *possible extent* $B^\Diamond$ are defined analogously. For $g \in G$ and $m \in M$ we use the abbreviations $g^\square$, $g^\Diamond$, $m^\square$ and $m^\Diamond$. For a incomplete contexts without "?" or formal context the certain and possible derivations and the usual derivation operator $\cdot'$ are the same, i.e., $A^\square = A^\Diamond = A'$.

Implications and Incomplete Contexts. We now recollect a notion of satisfiable implications in an incomplete context $\mathbb{K}$. Satisfiable implications of $\mathbb{K}$ are implications that have no counterexample in $\mathbb{K}$ and where a completion $\hat{\mathbb{K}}$ of $\mathbb{K}$ exists in which the implication holds. Formally, an attribute implication $R \to S$ is *satisfiable* in an incomplete context if $S \subseteq R^{\square\Diamond}$ (equivalent: if $\forall g \in G : R \subseteq g^\square \Rightarrow S \subseteq g^\Diamond$). For a premise R, the maximal satisfiable conclusion is $R^{\square\Diamond}$. It is the largest set of attributes that all objects, that certainly have all attributes in R, possibly have. The set of all satisfiable implications in an incomplete context $\mathbb{K}$ is denoted $\mathrm{Sat}(\mathbb{K})$.

Definition 2.2. *Let* $\mathbb{K} = (G, M, W, I)$ *be an incomplete context. Given a set of satisfiable implications* $\mathcal{L}$, *i.e.,* $\mathcal{L} \subseteq \mathrm{Sat}(\mathbb{K})$, *we define the* $\mathcal{L}$-*completion of* $\mathbb{K}$ *as the formal context* $\overline{\mathbb{K}} = (\overline{G}, M, J)$ *that is obtained by letting* $g^J = \mathcal{L}(g^\square)$ *for all* $g \in G$ *and adding a new object* h *to* $\overline{G}$ *for each model* $B \in \mathrm{Mod}\,\mathcal{L}$ *that is not yet an intent of an object in* G *such that* $h^J = B$.

Lemma 2.1. *Let* $\mathcal{L}$ *be a closed set of implications that is satisfiable in an incomplete context* $\mathbb{K}$. *Then* $\mathbb{K} \leq \overline{\mathbb{K}}$ *and* $\mathrm{Imp}(\overline{\mathbb{K}}) = \mathcal{L}$.

Proof. Because $\mathrm{Imp}((\mathrm{Mod}\,\mathcal{L}, M, \ni)) = \mathcal{L}$, by construction of $\overline{\mathbb{K}}$ it follows that $\mathrm{Imp}(\overline{\mathbb{K}}) = \mathcal{L}$. Further, for a closed and satisfiable set of implications $\mathcal{L}$ we have $\mathcal{L}(g^\square) \subseteq g^\Diamond$ for all $g \in G$ and thus $\mathbb{K} \leq \overline{\mathbb{K}}$. $\square$

3   Exploration with Multiple Experts

In this section, we examine the problem of attribute exploration with multiple experts. We introduce a formal representation of expert views and shared implications and study some of their properties. We provide an extension to the attribute exploration algorithm that allows for exploration of the shared implications of a group of experts and prove its correctness. In addition, we discuss the exploration of shared implications for some or all subsets of a group of experts.

Despite the development of many variants of and extensions to attribute exploration, the inclusion of multiple experts has only recently started to get some attention, c.f. [4,5,14,18]. However, in most of these works the underlying assumption is that there exists some true universe (for a given domain), i.e., there is no disagreement between the experts. The exception is [5], which introduces a triadic approach to attribute exploration and proposes a possible adaption to deal with multiple experts.

In this paper we expand on the ideas from [5] and give them a more general theoretical framework. In our setting we do not assume that the views of multiple experts must be compatible, i.e., two experts can disagree whether an object has an attribute or whether an implication holds in the domain. This can be the case when we have domains without an objectively *correct* view, for example, when dealing with opinions or other subjective properties. Non-compatible views can also arise, because real experts are normally not perfect and, even if there exists an objectively correct view of a domain, some experts might make mistakes, draw wrong conclusions or have some false ideas about the domain. The result, however, is always the same:

When we ask multiple experts, the answers we get can contain incompatible information. And, any attempt to combine the information to produce a single consistent answer to conform to the classic attribute exploration approach means we throw away part of the information and introduce some artifacts. When we talk about opinions the idea of combining opposing opinions clearly makes no sense. But, even if we know there exists some correct view of a domain, and we received answers with incompatible information it is usually impossible to deduce which information is correct and which is not. Hence, any resolution method without access to the correct information (assuming it exists) is bound to introduce information artifacts when attempting to merge incompatible answers.

Thus, in these cases it does not make sense to try and combine the information provided by multiple experts in order to obtain a more detailed view of the domain. Instead, we can try to find the parts of the domain where some or all of the experts agree, i.e., where they share some part of their view, and identify the conflicting parts. To this end we suggest attribute exploration of shared implications in order to examine the views of multiple domain experts.

Representing an Expert's View of a Domain. In our setting we do not assume the existence of some true (hidden) universe; and multiple views can have contradicting information.

We define a *domain* as a tuple $(\hat{G}, M)$ of finite sets of objects and attributes. A *complete view* on a domain is a pair $(\hat{\mathbb{K}}, \hat{\mathcal{L}})$ where $\hat{\mathbb{K}} = (\hat{G}, M, \hat{I})$ is a formal context and $\hat{\mathcal{L}}$ an implication theory on M such that $\hat{\mathcal{L}} = \text{Imp}(\hat{\mathbb{K}})$. A *partial view* (or simply *view*) on a domain is a pair $(\mathbb{K}, \mathcal{L})$ where $\mathbb{K} = (G, M, W, I)$ is an incomplete context and $\mathcal{L}$ an implication theory[3] on M such that there exists a complete view $(\hat{\mathbb{K}}, \hat{\mathcal{L}})$ with $\mathbb{K} \leq \hat{\mathbb{K}}$ and $\mathcal{L} = \hat{\mathcal{L}}$.

In a partial view $(\mathbb{K}, \mathcal{L})$ all implications in $\mathcal{L}$ are satisfiable in the context $\mathbb{K}$, i.e., $\mathcal{L} \subseteq \text{Sat}(\mathbb{K})$. Conversely, any pair of incomplete context $\mathbb{K}$ and implication theory $\mathcal{L} \subseteq \text{Sat}(\mathbb{K})$ is a partial view of the domain.

---

[3] Note that we consider $\mathcal{L}$ an implication theory because it is easier to work with. In practice we can use any set of implications where the closure is satisfiable in $\mathbb{K}$.

An *expert E_i for a domain* has a partial view $(\mathbb{K}_i, \mathcal{L}_i)$ of the domain where $\mathbb{K}_i = (G_i, M, W, I_i)$. In a group $\mathcal{E} = \{E_1, \ldots, E_k\}$ of experts each expert has a partial view of the domain. If we ask an expert E_i if an implication $R \to S$ holds in their view they answer in one of the following ways:

1. "Yes, $R \to S$ holds", if $R \to S \in \mathcal{L}_i$.
2. "No, $R \to S$ does not hold", if there is a counterexample g for $R \to S$ in $\mathbb{K}_i$.
3. "I do not know", if $R \to S$ has no counterexample in $\mathbb{K}_i$ and is not in $\mathcal{L}_i$.

This means in particular that we assume that an expert always provides the most informative answer that is consistent with their view on the domain.

Shared Implications. A *shared implication* of a group of experts $\mathcal{E}$ is an implication that holds in the view of all experts in $\mathcal{E}$. More precisely:

Definition 3.1. *Let $\mathcal{E} = \{E_1, \ldots, E_k\}$ be a group of experts where each expert E_i has a partial view $(\mathbb{K}_i, \mathcal{L}_i)$ of the domain. An attribute implication $R \to S$ holds for a group of experts $\mathcal{F} \subseteq \mathcal{E}$ if the implication holds in the view of each expert $E_i \in \mathcal{F}$, i.e., if $R \to S \in \mathcal{L}_i$ for all $E_i \in \mathcal{F}$. If $R \to S$ holds for the experts in $\mathcal{F}$ we call it a* shared implication *for $\mathcal{F}$.*

This is similar to the notion of *conditional implications* from triadic concept analysis (c.f. [5,9]) when we consider each experts view to correspond to one condition in the triadic setting.

Lemma 3.1. *Let $\mathcal{F} \subseteq \mathcal{E}$ be a group of experts with views $(\mathbb{K}_i, \mathcal{L}_i)$, then:*

1. *The set of shared implications for a group of experts $\mathcal{F} \subseteq \mathcal{E}$ is $\bigcap_{E_i \in \mathcal{F}} \mathcal{L}_i$. And, the implication theory of shared implications of a group of experts $\mathcal{F}$ is included in every implication theory of shared implications of subsets of $\mathcal{F}$.*
2. *An implication $R \to S$ holds in $\dot{\underset{E_i \in \mathcal{F}}{-}}\overline{\mathbb{K}}_i$ if and only if $R \to S$ is a shared implication for $\mathcal{F}$.*
3. *For each expert E_i there exists a complete view of the domain $(\hat{\mathbb{K}}_i, \mathcal{L}_i)$ with $\mathbb{K}_i \leq \hat{\mathbb{K}}_i \leq \overline{\mathbb{K}}_i$ (up to clarification of the contexts) and $\mathcal{L}_i = \mathrm{Imp}(\hat{\mathbb{K}}_i)$ and the shared implications of $\mathcal{F}$ are the implications which hold in the subposition context $\dot{\underset{E_i \in \mathcal{F}}{-}}\hat{\mathbb{K}}_i$.*

Proof. 1. follows directly from the definition of shared implication. Ad 2.: From Lemma 2.1 we know that $\mathrm{Imp}(\overline{\mathbb{K}}_i) = \mathcal{L}_i$ for each view. The implications that hold in $\dot{\underset{E_i \in \mathcal{F}}{-}}\overline{\mathbb{K}}_i$ are the implications that hold in each of the contexts $\overline{\mathbb{K}}_i$, hence, $\mathrm{Imp}(\dot{\underset{E_i \in \mathcal{F}}{-}}\overline{\mathbb{K}}_i) = \bigcap_{E_i \in \mathcal{F}} \mathcal{L}_i$. From 1. we know that $\bigcap_{E_i \in \mathcal{F}} \mathcal{L}_i$ are the shared implications for $\mathcal{F}$. Ad 3.: Since $\overline{\mathbb{K}}_i (\cong (\mathrm{Mod}\, \mathcal{L}_i, M, \ni))$ is (up to clarification) the largest context $\tilde{\mathbb{K}}_i$ such that $\mathbb{K}_i \leq \tilde{\mathbb{K}}_i$ and $\mathrm{Imp}(\tilde{\mathbb{K}}_i) = \mathcal{L}_i$, we have for every complete view $(\hat{\mathbb{K}}, \hat{\mathcal{L}})$ with $\hat{\mathcal{L}} = \mathcal{L}_i$ that $\mathbb{K}_i \leq \hat{\mathbb{K}} \leq \overline{\mathbb{K}}_i$. $\square$

Ordering Shared Implications. We utilize the notion of shared implications to hierarchically cluster the set of all attribute implications in the domain with respect to the experts in whose view they hold. To this end, we introduce the formal context of shared implications $\mathbb{C}^{\times} = (\mathrm{Imp}_M, \mathcal{E}, \models)$ where $(R \rightarrow S, E_i) \in \models :\Leftrightarrow R \rightarrow S$ holds in the view of E_i.

The concepts of $\mathbb{C}^{\times}$ are pairs $(\mathcal{L}, \mathcal{F})$ consisting of a set $\mathcal{L}$ of implications and a set $\mathcal{F}$ of experts such that the implications in $\mathcal{L}$ hold in the view of all experts in $\mathcal{F}$ and $\mathcal{L}$ is the largest set for which this is the case. The extents of the concepts of $\mathbb{C}^{\times}$ are precisely the implication theories of shared implications $\bigcap_{E_i \in F} \mathcal{L}_i$ for $\mathcal{F}$ where $\mathcal{F}$ is the corresponding group of experts from the intent.

The concept lattice of $\mathbb{C}^{\times}$ orders the shared implications with respect to the experts in whose view they hold. We call this the *system of shared implications*.

3.1   Explore Shared Implications

In the following we discuss the exploration of shared implications. We begin by considering how to adapt attribute exploration to obtain the shared implications for some group of experts $\mathcal{E}$. Then, we study how to efficiently explore the shared implications for some (or all) subsets of the group $\mathcal{E}$ of experts.

Explore Shared Implications for a Fixed Group of Experts. For a fixed group of experts $\mathcal{E}$ for a domain the exploration algorithm to obtain the relative canonical base of their shared implications is an adapted version of attribute exploration with background information and exceptions [19] and triadic exploration [5]. The universe of this exploration is the formal context $\mathbb{U} := \dotplus_{E_i \in \mathcal{E}} \overline{\mathbb{K}}_i$ where $\overline{\mathbb{K}}_i$ are the respective $\mathcal{L}$-completions of the partial views of the experts of the domain. Note, this universe is a theoretical aid to make use of the existing theory and is dependent on the views of the experts who participate in the exploration. In Algorithm 1 we present an implementation in pseudo-code.

Before the start of the algorithm, it is possible for the experts to provide some background information (a family K of example contexts and some known shared implications $\mathcal{L}_0$). We initialize $\mathcal{L}_{\mathbb{U}\mathcal{L}_0} := \emptyset$ and $\mathbb{C}$ as an empty context. Other information about the domain will be obtained by systematically asking the experts. In each iteration the algorithm determines the next question "Does $R \rightarrow R^{\square\lozenge}$ hold?" to pose, based on the known shared implications and already provided examples. More precisely, the premise R is the next relative pseudo-intent, i.e., the lectically smallest set R closed under the known shared implications and background implications that has a maximal satisfiable conclusion $R^{\square\lozenge}$ larger than R in the context of examples $\dotplus_{E_i \in \mathcal{E}} \mathbb{K}_i$. Then, each expert is asked which part of the conclusion follows from the premise and the answers are combined to determine the shared implication that holds for all experts. The shared implication is added to the set of shared implications $\mathcal{L}_{\mathbb{U}\mathcal{L}_0}$ and used to determine the next question. This process repeats until there is no question left, i.e., every implication can either be inferred from $\mathcal{L}_{\mathbb{U}\mathcal{L}_0}$ or the implication did

---

Algorithm 1: Explore the Shared Implications of a Group of Experts

---

    Input: The set of attributes M of the domain, a family of (possibly empty)
                incomplete contexts $K = \{\mathbb{K}_1, \ldots, \mathbb{K}_k\}$ containing examples given by
                the experts $\mathcal{E} = \{E_1, \ldots, E_k\}$ and a set $\mathcal{L}_0$ of background implications
                known to hold in the view of all experts (also possibly empty)
Interactive Input: $(\star)$ Each expert in $\mathcal{E}$ is asked which attributes in $R^{\square\Diamond}$
                        follow from R.
    Output: The $\mathcal{L}_0$-relative canonical base $\mathcal{L}_{\cup\mathcal{L}_0}$ of the shared implications, the
                family of (possibly enlarged) example contexts K and the context of
                shared implications $\mathbb{C}$

1 $\mathcal{L}_{\cup\mathcal{L}_0} := \emptyset$
2 $R := \emptyset$
3 $\mathbb{C} := (\emptyset, \{E_1, \ldots, E_k\}, \{\times, o, ?\}, \emptyset)$
4   **while** $R \neq M$ **do**
5   **while** $R \neq R^{\square\Diamond}$ *in* $\mathbb{K}$ *where*
6 $\mathbb{K} := (G, M, W, J) := \dot{\bigtimes}_{\mathbb{K}_i \in K} \mathbb{K}_i$
7   **do**
8   Ask each expert E_i which attributes $m \in R^{\square\Diamond}$ follow from R. $(\star)$
9   For each attribute $m \in R^{\square\Diamond}$, each expert E_i can respond with
             – "Yes, $R \to m$ holds."
             – "No, $R \to m$ does not hold", because object g is a counterexample.
                (which is added to $\mathbb{K}_i$ and thus to K)
             – "I do not know." (an artificial counterexample $g_{R \not\to m}$ is added to $\mathbb{K}_i$)
10 $S := \{m \in R^{\square\Diamond} |$ all experts responded that $R \to m$ holds$\}$
11   **if** $R \neq S$ **then** $\mathcal{L}_{\cup\mathcal{L}_0} := \mathcal{L}_{\cup\mathcal{L}_0} \cup \{R \to S\}$;   `// add shared implication`
13   Extend $\mathbb{C}$ with $R \to m$ for $m \in R^{\square\Diamond}$ and the respective answers given by
             the experts (i.e. one of $\{\times, o, ?\}$)
14   **end**
15 $R := \text{NextClosure}(R, M, \mathcal{L}_{\cup\mathcal{L}_0} \cup \mathcal{L}_0)$ `/* computes the next closure of` R
        `in` M `w.r.t. the implications` $\mathcal{L}_{\cup\mathcal{L}_0} \cup \mathcal{L}_0$`; c.f. [10, 11] */`
16 **end**
17 **return** $\mathcal{L}_{\cup\mathcal{L}_0}$, K and $\mathbb{C}$

---

not hold for some expert and a (possibly artificial) counterexample can be found
in one of the contexts in K.

    Note, that the algorithm also logs the answers given by the experts in the
context $\mathbb{C}$. This is not needed for Algorithm 1 but will be exploited in Algorithm 2
in order to prevent asking the same question multiple times when we explore the
domain with multiple subsets of experts, i. e., when we want to determine the
shared implications not just for one fixed group of experts, but for all possible
subsets of experts.

Theorem 3.1. *Let $\mathcal{E} = \{E_1, \ldots, E_k\}$ be a group of experts with partial views $(\mathbb{K}_i, \mathcal{L}_i)$. Let $\mathbb{U} = (G, M, I) = \dotplus_{E_i \in \mathcal{E}} \overline{\mathbb{K}}_i$ be the subposition context of the respective $\mathcal{L}_i$-completions of the experts' views of the domain. Then:*

1. *In Line 11 Algorithm 1 accepts only implications that are valid in $\mathbb{U}$.*
2. *In Line 11 1 adds a valid implication $R \to S$ to $\mathcal{L}_{\mathbb{U}\mathcal{L}_0}$ if and only if R is an $\mathcal{L}_0$-pseudo-intent and $S = R^{II}$.*

Proof. We prove Theorem 3.1 1. by contraposition. Assume that $R \to S$ is an implication that does not hold in $\mathbb{U}$. If $R \to S$ does not hold in $\mathbb{U}$ then there is an object $g \in \overline{\mathbb{K}}_i$ in some $\mathcal{L}_i$-completion $\overline{\mathbb{K}}_i$ that is a counterexample to the implication. Since $\mathrm{Imp}(\overline{\mathbb{K}}_i) = \mathcal{L}_i$ it follows that $R \to S \notin \mathcal{L}_i$. Hence, given the question "Does $R \to S$ hold?" the expert E_i does not accept the implication as valid. Therefore, S is not accepted to follow from R by all experts and is not accepted as a shared implication in Line 11 of Algorithm 1.

The proof of Theorem 3.1 2. is similar to that of [10, Prop. 34]. We prove this by induction over the premise size k of R. We begin with the base case $R = \emptyset$.

"⇒": An implication $R \to S$ is added to $\mathcal{L}_{\mathbb{U}\mathcal{L}_0}$ if the conclusion S is maximal and $S \neq R$, i.e., if $S = R^{II}$ and $R \neq R^{II}$. Hence, $\emptyset \to S$ is added to $\mathcal{L}_{\mathbb{U}\mathcal{L}_0}$ if $S = \emptyset^{II}$ and $\emptyset \neq \emptyset^{II}$ and thus, $\emptyset$ is an $\mathcal{L}_0$-pseudo-intent.

"⇐": Now let $\emptyset$ be an $\mathcal{L}_0$-pseudo-intent. The implication $\emptyset \to \emptyset^{II}$ holds by definition. It is added to $\mathcal{L}_{\mathbb{U}\mathcal{L}_0}$ because $\emptyset^{II}$ is the largest set for which all experts agree that it follows from $\emptyset$, and $\emptyset \neq \emptyset^{II}$ by definition of $\mathcal{L}_0$-pseudo-intent.

Assume now that the proposition holds for all subsets N of M with $|N| \leq k$.

"⇒": Let $R \to S$ be a valid implication in $\mathbb{K}$ with $|R| = k + 1$ and added to $\mathcal{L}_{\mathbb{U}\mathcal{L}_0}$. We show that (i) $S = R^{II}$ and that (ii) R is an $\mathcal{L}_0$-pseudo-intent. Ad (i): Assume that there exists $m \in R^{\square\Diamond} \setminus R^{II}$. Then some expert does not confirm (with "yes") that the attribute follows from R and a (real or artificial) counterexample is added. Thus we have $S = R^{II}$. Because the implication is added to $\mathcal{L}_{\mathbb{U}\mathcal{L}_0}$, we have $R \neq R^{II}$. Ad (ii): Assume R is not an $\mathcal{L}_0$-pseudo-intent. Then at least one of the properties of the definition of $\mathcal{L}_0$-pseudo-intent does not hold. We show that each case yields a contradiction ($\lightning$). If R does not respect $\mathcal{L}_0$ then R is not suggested as premise because it is not $(\mathcal{L}_{\mathbb{U}\mathcal{L}_0} \cup \mathcal{L}_0)$-closed and $R \to S$ can not be added to $\mathcal{L}_{\mathbb{U}\mathcal{L}_0}$. $\lightning$ If $R = R^{II}$ then $R \to R^{II}$ can not be added to $\mathcal{L}_{\mathbb{U}\mathcal{L}_0}$. $\lightning$ If there exists an $\mathcal{L}_0$-pseudo-intent $P \subset R$ with $P^{II} \not\subseteq R$ then $P \to P^{II}$ is in $\mathcal{L}_{\mathbb{U}\mathcal{L}_0}$ by induction hypothesis and because implications are added to $\mathcal{L}_{\mathbb{U}\mathcal{L}_0}$ in lectic order with respect to their premises. But then R is not $(\mathcal{L}_{\mathbb{U}\mathcal{L}_0} \cup \mathcal{L}_0)$-closed and is not suggested as premise by the algorithm and thus, $R \to S$ can not be added to $\mathcal{L}_{\mathbb{U}\mathcal{L}_0}$. $\lightning$ Hence, R is an $\mathcal{L}_0$-pseudo-intent.

"⇐": Now let R be an $\mathcal{L}_0$-pseudo-intent with $|R| = k + 1$. We show that $R \to R^{II}$ is added to $\mathcal{L}_{\mathbb{U}\mathcal{L}_0}$. For any implication $P \to Q$ in $\mathcal{L}_{\mathbb{U}\mathcal{L}_0}$ with $P \subset R$ we have by the induction hypothesis that P is an $\mathcal{L}_0$-pseudo-intent and $Q = P^{II}$. Because R is an $\mathcal{L}_0$-pseudo-intent we have $P^{II} \subseteq R$. Hence, R is $(\mathcal{L}_{\mathbb{U}\mathcal{L}_0} \cup \mathcal{L}_0)$-closed and the implication $R \to R^{\square\Diamond}$ will be suggested to the experts. Then R^{II} is the maximal set of attributes for which all experts agree that it follows from R since for every other attribute $R^{\square\Diamond} \setminus R^{II}$ some expert has a counterexample. By definition of $\mathcal{L}_0$-pseudo-intent we have $R \neq R^{II}$ and the implication $R \to R^{II}$ is added to $\mathcal{L}_{U \mathcal{L}_0}$. □

Corollary 3.1. *Upon termination of Algorithm 1, the output $\mathcal{L}_{U \mathcal{L}_0}$ is the canonical base of $\mathbb{U} = \dot{\sqsupset}_{E_i \in \mathcal{E}} \overline{\mathbb{K}}_i$ relative to $\mathcal{L}_0$, and $\mathcal{L}_{U \mathcal{L}_0} \cup \mathcal{L}_0$ is a base of $\bigcap_{E_i \in \mathcal{E}} \mathcal{L}_i$. Further, $\forall R \subseteq M$ we have R^{II} (in $\mathbb{U}$) $= R^{\square \lozenge}$ (in $\mathbb{K}$) at the end of the exploration.*

Proof. This follows from Theorem 3.1 and Theorem 3.1. □

Explore the System of Shared Implications. Now that we know how to obtain the shared implications for some group of experts $\mathcal{E}$, let us consider how to obtain the shared implication theories for some or all subsets of $\mathcal{E}$. Essentially, the goal is to obtain the concept lattice of the context of shared implications $\mathbb{C}^\times$.

From [5] we know that there are several viable strategies: One option is to explore the domain for each expert separately, i.e., obtain the columns of $\mathbb{C}^\times$, then combine the results to obtain the context $\mathbb{C}^\times$ and from this compute the concept lattice $\mathfrak{B}(\mathbb{C}^\times)$. This has the advantage that we can parallelize the individual explorations because there is no coordination overhead during the exploration step. However, this also means that we need all explorations to be finished before we obtain any results. In particular, if we are only interested in the shared implications of all experts or only of a subset of $\mathfrak{B}(\mathbb{C}^\times)$, this approach usually asks more questions than necessary.

Another option is to explore the lattice $\mathfrak{B}(\mathbb{C}^\times)$ from bottom to top, i.e., explore the shared implications for all non-empty expert subsets of $\mathcal{E}$ from largest to smallest, and reduce the amount of questions in later explorations by using the already discovered shared implications as background information. This approach has some coordination overhead and the explorations can only be parallelized for explorations with the same number of experts. But, it also has the advantage that only the questions necessary to find the shared implications of interest are posed. In particular, we do not need to explore all of $\mathfrak{B}(\mathbb{C}^\times)$ if we are only interested in some subset of the system of shared implications. In Algorithm 2 we provide an implementation of this approach in pseudo-code.

No matter which approach is chosen, we need to consider how to merge the results of multiple explorations with different subset of experts. In order to merge the example contexts for each expert we use the incomplete context supremum. Since a single expert's view is consistent for multiple explorations the example contexts for this expert do not contain any contradicting information and the supremum context exists. The contexts of shared implications can also be merged using the incomplete context supremum. The supremum always exists because the answers from each expert are consistent across multiple explorations. Joining contexts of shared implications introduces some "?" in the context because not all experts have responded to all questions from all explorations. However, some of these might be answered using other responses given by an expert; either because they follow from the accepted implications or because some given example contradicts the validity of the implication. Therefore, after merging multiple

---

Algorithm 2: Explore the System of Shared Implications

Input: A family of (possibly empty) incomplete contexts $K = \{\mathbb{K}_1, \ldots, \mathbb{K}_k\}$ containing examples given by the experts $\mathcal{E} = \{E_1, \ldots, E_k\}$, a context $\mathbb{C} = (G_\mathbb{C}, \mathcal{E}, I_\mathbb{C})$ of shared implications (also possibly empty).

Output: A possibly enlarged family of examples K and the context of shared implications $\mathbb{C}$ which contains the experts responses.

1 **for** $\tilde{\mathcal{E}}$ *in linear extension of* $(\mathcal{P}(\mathcal{E}) \setminus \emptyset, \supseteq)$ **do**
2 | $\tilde{K}$ = subset of K corresponding to the experts in $\tilde{\mathcal{E}}$
3 | $\tilde{\mathcal{L}} = \tilde{\mathcal{E}}^\square$ (in $\mathbb{C}$)
4 | $\hat{\mathcal{L}}, \hat{K}, \hat{\mathbb{C}}$ = explore-shared-implications($M, \tilde{K}, \tilde{\mathcal{E}}, \tilde{\mathcal{L}}$)
5 | merge $\hat{K}$ into K
6 | merge $\hat{\mathbb{C}}$ into $\mathbb{C}$ and ?-reduce where possible
7 **end**
8 **return** $\mathbb{C}$, K

---

contexts of shared implications in a second step we check if some of the newly introduced "?" can be inferred from already obtained information.

3.2 Improving Collaboration

If we assume that experts for a domain want to reach a more detailed view of the domain the suggested approach of only exploring their shared views is insufficient. However, once some shared views are explored we can use the obtained information to examine the conflicts, inconsistencies and unknowns, for example:

- Implications which only have artificial counterexamples.
- Implications which are accepted by most experts and unknown to or rejected by only a few.
- Controversial object attribute relations, i.e., relations that are accepted by some experts and rejected by others.
- Implications and examples that conflict with each other for any two experts.

This helps a group of experts find a larger common ground and allows them to address some of the sources of disagreement. We do not believe, however, that the exploration procedure would benefit from incorporating a conflict resolution step. Rather, the exploration serves as a means to establish a baseline of commonalities, to make disagreements visible and to enable further cooperation. Discussion and potential resolution of conflicts should be a second, separate step.

4 Conclusion and Outlook

We have expanded on ideas for attribute exploration with multiple domain experts raised in [5] and provided a theoretical framework which builds on a multitude of previous works in the realm of formal concept analysis. The resulting attribute exploration algorithm is an extension of attribute exploration that allows for multiple experts, incomplete information and background information.

Our approach serves as a step towards collaborative exploration for domains where experts might hold conflicting views. An exploration of the shared views of a group of experts provides a structured approach to uncovering commonalities and differences in the experts views and can serve as a baseline for further investigations. An example for the exploration of shared views is provided in the arXiv version of the paper, see Footnote 3. As a next step, we will examine the properties of the two proposed approaches to explore $\mathfrak{B}(\mathbb{C}^\times)$ in more detail, in particular with respect to the required expert input.

References

1. Belnap, N.D.: A useful four-valued logic. In: Dunn, J.M., Epstein, G. (eds.) Modern Uses of Multiple-Valued Logic. Episteme, vol. 2, pp. 5–37. Springer, Dordrecht (1977). https://doi.org/10.1007/978-94-010-1161-7_2
2. Burmeister, P.: Merkmalimplikationen bei unvollständigem wissen. In: Lex, W. (ed.) Arbeitstagung Begriffsanalyse und Künstliche Intelligenz, pp. 15–46. No. 89/3 in Informatik-Bericht, Clausthal-Zellerfeld (1991)
3. Burmeister, P., Holzer, R.: On the treatment of incomplete knowledge in formal concept analysis. In: Ganter, B., Mineau, G.W. (eds.) ICCS-ConceptStruct 2000. LNCS (LNAI), vol. 1867, pp. 385–398. Springer, Heidelberg (2000). https://doi.org/10.1007/10722280_27
4. Felde, M., Stumme, G.: Interactive collaborative exploration using incomplete contexts. CoRR abs/1908.08740 (2019)
5. Felde, M., Stumme, G.: Triadic exploration and exploration with multiple experts. In: Braud, A., Buzmakov, A., Hanika, T., Le Ber, F. (eds.) ICFCA 2021. LNCS (LNAI), vol. 12733, pp. 175–191. Springer, Cham (2021). https://doi.org/10.1007/978-3-030-77867-5_11
6. Fitting, M.: Kleene's logic, generalized. Logic Comput. 1(6), 797–810 (1991)
7. Ganter, B.: Two basic algorithms in concept analysis. In: Kwuida, L., Sertkaya, B. (eds.) ICFCA 2010. LNCS (LNAI), vol. 5986, pp. 312–340. Springer, Heidelberg (2010). https://doi.org/10.1007/978-3-642-11928-6_22
8. Ganter, B.: Attribute exploration with background knowledge. Theoret. Comput. Sci. 217(2), 215–233 (1999)
9. Ganter, B., Obiedkov, S.: Implications in triadic formal contexts. In: Wolff, K.E., Pfeiffer, H.D., Delugach, H.S. (eds.) ICCS-ConceptStruct 2004. LNCS (LNAI), vol. 3127, pp. 186–195. Springer, Heidelberg (2004). https://doi.org/10.1007/978-3-540-27769-9_12
10. Ganter, B., Obiedkov, S.: More expressive variants of exploration. In: Conceptual Exploration, pp. 237–292. Springer, Heidelberg (2016). https://doi.org/10.1007/978-3-662-49291-8_6
11. Ganter, B., Wille, R.: Formal Concept Analysis: Mathematical Foundations. Springer, Heidelberg (1999). https://doi.org/10.1007/978-3-642-59830-2
12. Ginsberg, M.L.: Multivalued logics: a uniform approach to reasoning in artificial intelligence. Comput. Intell. 4(3), 265–316 (1988)

13. Guigues, J.L., Duquenne, V.: Familles minimales d'implications informatives résultant d'un tableau de données binaires. Mathématiques et Sciences Humaines **95**, 5–18 (1986)
14. Hanika, T., Zumbrägel, J.: Towards collaborative conceptual exploration. In: Chapman, P., Endres, D., Pernelle, N. (eds.) ICCS 2018. LNCS (LNAI), vol. 10872, pp. 120–134. Springer, Cham (2018). https://doi.org/10.1007/978-3-319-91379-7_10
15. Holzer, R.: Methoden der formalen Begriffsanalyse bei der Behandlung unvollständigen Wissens. Dissertation, TU Darmstadt, Shaker (2001)
16. Holzer, R.: Knowledge acquisition under incomplete knowledge using methods from formal concept analysis: Part I. Fund. Inform. **63**(1), 17–39 (2004)
17. Holzer, R.: Knowledge acquisition under incomplete knowledge using methods from formal concept analysis: Part II. Fund. Inform. **63**(1), 41–63 (2004)
18. Kriegel, F.: Parallel attribute exploration. In: Haemmerlé, O., Stapleton, G., Faron Zucker, C. (eds.) ICCS 2016. LNCS (LNAI), vol. 9717, pp. 91–106. Springer, Cham (2016). https://doi.org/10.1007/978-3-319-40985-6_8
19. Stumme, G.: Attribute exploration with background implications and exceptions. In: Bock, H.H., Polasek, W. (eds.) Data Analysis and Information Systems. Statistical and Conceptual Approaches. Proceedings GfKl 1995. Studies in Classification, Data Analysis, and Knowledge Organization, vol. 7. pp. 457–469. Springer, Heidelberg (1996). https://doi.org/10.1007/978-3-642-80098-6_39
20. Wille, R.: Restructuring lattice theory: an approach based on hierarchies of concepts. In: Rival, I. (ed.) Ordered Sets, pp. 445–470. Springer, Dordrecht (1982). https://doi.org/10.1007/978-94-009-7798-3_15

Orbital Concept Lattices

Jens Kötters[✉] and Stefan E. Schmidt

Institut für Algebra, Technische Universität Dresden, Dresden, Germany
jkoetters5@gmail.com, stefan.schmidt@tu-dresden.de

Abstract. The paper introduces orbital concept lattices, which enhance concept lattices of relational structures with a semigroup action that encodes projection, renaming and duplication operations on concept extents, and fuses them with their counterparts on concept intents (formalized by tableau queries). This strengthens the existing connections between this branch of FCA and database theory, and it opens up a new possibility of characterizing such concept lattices by a set of axioms. The orbital semilattices, also introduced in this paper, are a first step in this direction, as they characterize the subsemilattices generated by finite queries, and thereby also enable a connection with algebraic logic.

Keywords: Relational algebra · Database theory · Cylindric algebra · Lattice theory

1 Motivation

Concept lattices of relational structures [10] form the basis of a connection between Formal Concept Analysis (FCA) and database theory. While the formalism in the original paper still has an intuitive flavor, the connections of the concept model to both database theory and formal logic have been made formally explicit in [12, Sects. 3,4]. The "Alice book" by Abiteboul et al. [1], in particular, serves as an inspiration for how the connection between FCA and database theory could be deepened, so that the idea of formal concepts could be made more appealing to the database theory community.

An observation about the nature of concept intents (see the beginning of Sect. 3) reveals that the projection and renaming operations of the SPJR algebra [1] can be lifted to the level of concepts; while these operations apply to concept extents, they have meaningful counterparts on concept intents, where they correspond to existential quantification and one-to-one variable substitution. This creates an idea of concepts as a formalism that unifies relational algebra (via concept intents) and relational calculus (via concept intents), or at least the parts that pertain to conjunctive queries, i.e. SPJR algebra and the conjunctive calculus [1].

With the given formalization of concepts, it is natural to represent the two operations as special cases of a semigroup action (originally a monoid action was used), which could be roughly seen as a kind of scalar multiplication, and an

T. Braun et al. (Eds.): ICCS 2022, LNCS 13403, pp. 66–81, 2022.
https://doi.org/10.1007/978-3-031-16663-1_6

analysis (cf. Sect. 3.4) shows that the semigroup action represents exactly three operations, the third being column duplication (from an extensional point of view).

Because the semigroup action generates some kind of orbits (cf. Sect. 6), the concept lattice with the additional operation(s) is referred to as an *orbital concept lattice*. With the new operation(s) on hand, the question of an axiomatic characterization for concept lattices of relational structures becomes accessible. For that purpose, it is useful to also make the notions of domain (a distinctive feature of these concepts) and diagonals (a notion from cylindric algebra [8]) available.

A first result, which characterizes such concept lattices for finite data, was presented at the AAA98 workshop in Dresden. The flaw of this characterization, apart from two smaller mistakes, was that the condition that characterizes finiteness was particularly ugly, unsuitable for a set of axioms. The question was then, whether the remaining axioms are sufficient to characterize the general case (where data can be infinite). It turned out that the only axiom making a statement about the supremum (apart from the basic lattice axioms) could be derived from the other axioms! So it seems that, intrinsically, the axioms characterize semilattices. The axioms for orbital semilattices, presented in Sect. 4, are a reshaped version of these original axioms, with the condition for lattice completeness dropped. While the original question (an axiomatization of the concept lattices) is still open, the significance of orbital semilattices is presented in this paper.

2   Recap: Connecting FCA and Database Theory

This section is a summary of [12, Sects. 3–5], with slight modifications.

2.1   Variables and Named Tuples

Throughout the paper, $\mathbf{var} = \{x_1, x_2, \dots\}$ denotes a countably infinite set of variables; and x_i always denotes the i-th variable of the indicated enumeration. A *named tuple* over a set G is a function $t \in G^X$ defined on a finite set $X \subseteq \mathbf{var}$, i.e. $X \in \mathfrak{P}_{\text{fin}}(\mathbf{var})$. For arbitrary $y_1, \dots, y_n \in \mathbf{var}$, we may write $t \in G^{\{y_1, \dots, y_n\}}$ in the named tuple notation $\langle y_1{:}t(y_1), \dots, y_n{:}t(y_n)\rangle$, with $y_1, \dots, y_n$ in any order; in particular, $\langle\rangle \in G^{\emptyset}$ is the *empty tuple*. The set

$$\mathrm{NTup}(G) := \bigcup \{G^X \mid X \in \mathfrak{P}_{\text{fin}}(\mathbf{var})\} \tag{1}$$

contains all named tuples over G. Given $t_1, t_2 \in \mathrm{NTup}(G)$, we say that t_2 *extends* t_1, written $t_1 \leq t_2$, if t_2 extends t_1 as a function. We write $t = t_1 \oplus t_2$ if t combines t_1 and t_2 (i.e., for $t_1 \in G^{X_1}$ and $t_2 \in G^{X_2}$, if $t \in G^{X_1 \cup X_2}$ and $t_1 \leq t$ and $t_2 \leq t$).

J. Kötters and S. E. Schmidt

2.2 Tables

A *table* with *schema* $X \in \mathfrak{P}_{\text{fin}}(\mathbf{var})$ and *entries* in G is a non-empty set $T \subseteq G^X$ (the named tuples in T are the table's *rows*). In addition, there is the *empty table*, represented by the empty set; it is assigned the infinite schema $\mathbf{var}$. The set

$$\text{Tab}(G) := \bigcup \{\mathfrak{P}(G^X) \mid X \in \mathfrak{P}_{\text{fin}}(\mathbf{var})\} \tag{2}$$

contains all tables with entries in G. A *table order* is defined on any table set $\text{Tab}(G)$ as follows: If T_1 and T_2 are tables with schema X_1 and X_2, respectively, then $T_1 \leq T_2$ if and only if $X_2 \subseteq X_1$ and $\{t|_{X_2} \mid t \in T_1\} \subseteq T_2$. For $X_1 = X_2$, the table order is simply the subset relation; the empty table, which has schema $\mathbf{var}$, is the bottom element; and the table $\{\langle\rangle\}$, which has schema $\emptyset$, is the top element. The table order has a well-known infimum operation: The *natural join*, defined by $T_1 \bowtie T_2 := \{t \in G^{X_1 \cup X_2} \mid t|_{X_1} \in T_1 \text{ and } t|_{X_2} \in T_2\}$ for tables $T_1, T_2 \in \text{Tab}(G)$ with schemas X_1, X_2, respectively. Tables can be understood as compact representations of sets, namely

$$\text{pset}(T) := \{t \in \text{NTup}(G) \mid t|_X \in T\}, \tag{3}$$

for a table $T \in \text{Tab}(G)$ with schema X. This gives a better understanding of the table order: $\text{pset} : (\text{Tab}(G), \leq) \to (\mathfrak{P}(\text{NTup}(G)), \subseteq)$ is an order embedding, which identifies the table order with set inclusion, and natural join with set intersection (see [12, Sect. 3.5 f.]). Imieliński and Lipski [9] have used a similar embedding h, for connecting Codd's relational data model to cylindric algebra. The table order $(\text{Tab}(G), \leq)$ is a complete lattice [12, Sect. 3.5]; the supremum of $T_1 \subseteq G^{X_1}$ and $T_2 \subseteq G^{X_2}$ is the *co-join* $T_1 \boxtimes T_2 := \{t|_{X_2} \mid t \in X_1\} \cup \{t|_{X_1} \mid t \in X_2\}$.

2.3 Relational Structures

A *relational signature* is a set M of relation symbols. Each symbol has an *arity* $n \in \mathbb{N}_{\geq 1}$, and $M_n \subseteq M$ denotes the subset of all n-ary relation symbols. A *relational structure* over M, or an *M-structure*, is a pair $\mathcal{G} = (A, \mathfrak{a})$ consisting of an *underlying set* $|\mathcal{G}| := A$ and a function $\mathfrak{a} : M \to \bigcup_{n \geq 1} \mathfrak{P}(A^n)$, which assigns a relation $m^{\mathcal{G}} := \mathfrak{a}(m) \subseteq A^n$ to each symbol $m \in M_n$. A homomorphism $\varphi : \mathcal{G} \to \mathcal{H}$ of M-structures is a function $\varphi : |\mathcal{G}| \to |\mathcal{H}|$ such that $(g_1, \dots, g_n) \in m^{\mathcal{G}}$ implies $(\varphi(g_1), \dots, \varphi(g_n)) \in m^{\mathcal{H}}$ for all $m \in M_n$ and $n \geq 1$.

2.4 Tableau Queries

A *tableau query* over M is a pair $(\mathcal{G}, \nu)$ consisting of an M-structure $\mathcal{G}$ and a *window* $\nu \in \text{NTup}(|\mathcal{G}|)$; conventionally, ν is called the *summary* of the query [1]. We may use graph theoretic terminology for tableau queries: each $a \in |\mathcal{G}|$ is a *node*, and each $(a_1, \dots, a_n) \in r^{\mathcal{G}}$, for $r \in M_n$, is an *edge* of arity n (more specifically an *r-edge*). Figure 1 shows a tableau query $(\mathcal{G}, \nu)$ over the signature $\{m, r\}$, where m is a unary symbol, and r is a quaternary symbol, moreover

$|\mathcal{G}| = \{a, b, c\}$, $m^{\mathcal{G}} = \{(a), (b)\}$, $r^{\mathcal{G}} = \{(a, b, b, a)\}$ and $\nu = \langle x_1{:}a, x_2{:}c, x_3{:}c \rangle$. An n-ary edge $(a_1, \ldots, a_n)$ is drawn as a rectangle, which is connected to each a_i by an i-labeled line; we represent $\nu(x_i) = a_i$ by drawing a bold x_i next to a_i and, for additional emphasis, mark the node a_i yellow. If all edges are unary or binary, a more conventional (and economic) graph notation may be used: a binary s-edge (a_1, a_2) is drawn as an s-labeled arrow from a_1 to a_2 (cf. Fig. 4), and a unary p-edge (a) as a node label p. A *star query* is a query that consists of n nodes, connected by a single n-ary edge, or just an isolated node (Fig. 2), with a bijective window; a discussion of star queries has to be deferred to Sect. 3.5.

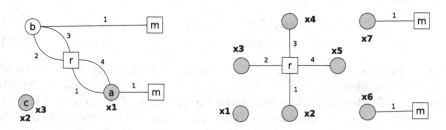

Fig. 1. Tableau query   **Fig. 2.** Star queries

A tableau query is *finite* if it has a finite number of nodes and edges. We write $\mathrm{CQ}(M)$ for the class of all (finite or infinite) tableau queries over M.

A homomorphism $\varphi : (\mathcal{G}_1, \nu_1) \to (\mathcal{G}_2, \nu_2)$ of tableau queries is a homomorphism $\varphi : \mathcal{G}_1 \to \mathcal{G}_2$ which preserves the subjects of the query, i.e. which satisfies $\varphi \circ \nu_1 \leq \nu_2$. We write $(\mathcal{G}_1, \nu_1) \lesssim (\mathcal{G}_2, \nu_2)$ if a homomorphism $\varphi : (\mathcal{G}_1, \nu_1) \to (\mathcal{G}_2, \nu_2)$ exists. This defines a preorder on $\mathrm{CQ}(M)$ called the *homomorphism preorder*. If $Q_1 \lesssim Q_2$, then Q_1 is more *general* (or less *specific*) than Q_2; if both $Q_1 \lesssim Q_2$ and $Q_2 \lesssim Q_1$, then Q_1 and Q_2 are *hom-equivalent*, and we denote this by $Q_1 \simeq Q_2$. A reader familiar with category theory may note that universal products and co-products are infima and suprema, respectively, in the homomorphism preorder (unique up to hom-equivalence). The *(direct) product* $\prod_{i \in I} Q_i$ and the *sum* $\sum_{i \in I} Q_i$ of tableau queries (for details cf. [12, Sect. 4]) are the product and co-product in the sense of category theory; i.e. the preordered class $(\mathrm{CQ}(M), \lesssim)$ has the properties of a complete lattice, in that every subset has an infimum and a supremum. We write $Q_1 \times Q_2$ and $Q_1 + Q_2$ for the binary product and sum, respectively. The sum $(\mathcal{G}_1, \nu_1) + (\mathcal{G}_2, \nu_2)$ is best described in terms of graphs: we place the graphs for $(\mathcal{G}_1, \nu_1)$ and $(\mathcal{G}_2, \nu_2)$ side by side, and then merge $\nu_1(x)$ with $\nu_2(x)$, for all x where both $\nu_1(x)$ and $\nu_2(x)$ are defined. The smallest element in $(\mathrm{CQ}(M), \lesssim)$ is the *tautology* $\mathsf{true} := ((\emptyset, (\emptyset)_{m \in M}), \langle \rangle)$. We introduce a new greatest element false, called the *contradiction*, which is not an element of $\mathrm{CQ}(M)$, and set $\mathrm{CQ}_\perp(M) := \mathrm{CQ}(M) \cup \{\mathsf{false}\}$. For a summary, we note that $(\mathrm{CQ}_\perp(M), +, \times, \mathsf{true}, \mathsf{false})$ is a (class-based) bounded lattice, which is complete in the above sense.

2.5   Result Operation

A *database* with schema M is an M-structure Δ, and we call the elements of
$G := |\Delta|$ the *objects* of Δ. The relations of Δ might correspond one-to-one with
the tables of a relational database; we suggest a more flexible approach, where Δ
is derived from a database by conceptual/relational scaling [11] (in a database
with tables Author and Book, the elements of G would then be authors and
books); but ultimately, Δ can be any kind of relational data.

Every database Δ with schema M comes with an operation $\mathrm{res}_\Delta :$
$\mathrm{CQ}_\perp(M) \to \mathrm{Tab}(G)$, which assigns a *result table* to each query. Concretely,
we define

$$\mathrm{res}_\Delta(\mathcal{G}, \nu) := \mathrm{Hom}(\mathcal{G}, \Delta) \circ \nu, \tag{4}$$
$$\mathrm{res}_\Delta(\text{false}) := \emptyset \tag{5}$$

for all $(\mathcal{G}, \nu) \in \mathrm{CQ}(M)$, treating false separately; $\mathrm{Hom}(\mathcal{G}, \Delta)$ in (4) is the set
of homomorphisms from $\mathcal{G}$ to Δ, so $\mathrm{res}_\Delta(\mathcal{G}, \nu) = \{\varphi \circ \nu \mid \varphi : \mathcal{G} \to \Delta\}$. We
have $\nu \in \mathcal{G}^X$ for some $X \in \mathfrak{P}_{\mathrm{fin}}(\mathbf{var})$; the elements of X are called the *free
variables* (or *subject variables*) of $(\mathcal{G}, \nu)$, since the rows of $\mathrm{res}_\Delta(\mathcal{G}, \nu)$ are the
possible assignments to the variables in X. More formally, $\mathrm{free}(\mathcal{G}, \nu) := X$ and

$$\mathrm{schema}(\mathrm{res}_\Delta(Q)) = \begin{cases} \mathrm{free}(Q) & \text{if } \mathrm{res}_\Delta(Q) \neq \emptyset \\ \mathbf{var} & \text{otherwise} \end{cases}. \tag{6}$$

The homomorphism theorem [1, Sect. 6.2] is a central result in database theory,
whereby containment of tableau queries (i.e. query implication) is characterized
by homomorphism. It is usually stated for queries in the same free variables,
but can be generalized to arbitrary queries in $\mathrm{CQ}_\perp(M)$. The homomorphism
theorem (in its generalized form [12, Thm. 2]) states that,

$$(\mathcal{G}_1, \nu_1) \lesssim (\mathcal{G}_2, \nu_2) :\Leftrightarrow \begin{array}{l} \mathrm{res}_\Delta(\mathcal{G}_2, \nu_2) \leq \mathrm{res}_\Delta(\mathcal{G}_1, \nu_1) \\ \text{for all relational structures } \Delta. \end{array} \tag{7}$$

It makes sense to consider $(\mathcal{G}_1, \nu_1)$ and $(\mathcal{G}_2, \nu_2)$ *equivalent* if $\mathrm{res}_\Delta(\mathcal{G}_1, \nu) = \mathrm{res}_\Delta(\mathcal{G}_2, \nu)$ for all Δ. As (7) shows, this notion of equivalence coincides with
hom-equivalence.

A non-empty finite tableau query corresponds to a logical formula [12, Sect. 3]
For an example, consider the query $(\mathcal{G}, \nu)$ in Fig. 1. It has the free variables x_1,
x_2 and x_3. The nodes a, b and c correspond to existentially quantified variables
$z_a, z_b, z_c \in \mathbf{var} \setminus \{x_1, x_2, x_3\}$; the three edges translate to atoms $r(z_a, z_b, z_b, z_a)$,
$m(z_b)$ and $m(z_a)$; the isolated node to an equality atom $z_c = z_c$; and the win-
dow $\nu = \langle x_1 : a, x_2 : c, x_3 : c \rangle$ to the equality atoms $x_1 = z_a$, $x_2 = z_c$ and $x_3 = z_c$. So
$\exists z_a \exists z_b \exists z_c (r(z_a, z_b, z_b, z_a) \wedge m(z_b) \wedge m(z_a) \wedge z_c = z_c \wedge x_1 = z_a \wedge x_2 = z_c \wedge x_3 = z_c)$ represents $(\mathcal{G}, \nu)$ as a formula. Abiteboul et al. [1] allow constants in tableau queries,
but as shown above, we only allow variables. A way around this limitation is to
encode constants as unary relation symbols.

Logically, the sum $Q_1 + Q_2$ of queries is the conjunction $\varphi_{Q_1} \wedge \varphi_{Q_2}$ of their
formulas; for the product $Q_1 \times Q_2$ there is no simple analogy.

The *equality query* $\mathcal{E}(x,y) := ((\{a\}, (\emptyset)_{m\in M}), \langle x{:}a, y{:}a\rangle)$, where $x, y \in$ **var** and a arbitrary, produces the *equality table* $E(x,y) := \{\langle x{:}g, y{:}g\rangle \mid g \in G\}$, i.e.

$$\mathrm{res}_\Delta(\mathcal{E}(x,y)) = E(x,y), \tag{8}$$

in every Δ. As a special case, $\mathcal{E}(x,x) = ((\{a\}, (\emptyset)_{m\in M}), \langle x{:}a\rangle)$ produces a list of all objects in G, returned in a table $E(x,x)$ which has the single column x. Notably, for $x \neq y$, we have $E(x,x) \neq E(y,y)$ in every non-empty Δ, so the queries $\mathcal{E}(x,x)$ and $\mathcal{E}(y,y)$ are not equivalent. In this, *table semantics* differs from standard predicate logical semantics, where $x{=}x$ and $y{=}y$ are equivalent.

A few more properties of the result operation: from (7) follows that $\mathrm{res}_\Delta :$ $(\mathrm{CQ}(M), \lesssim) \to (\mathrm{Tab}(G), \leq)$ is antitone; moreover, we have

$$\mathrm{res}_\Delta(\mathsf{true}) = \{\langle\rangle\}, \tag{9}$$

$$\mathrm{res}_\Delta(Q_1 + Q_2) = \mathrm{res}_\Delta(Q_1) \bowtie \mathrm{res}_\Delta(Q_2), \tag{10}$$

where (9) is easy to check; for (10) see [12, eq. (56)].

2.6 Concepts

For any relational structure Δ with object set G and signature M, the function $\mathrm{res}_\Delta : (\mathrm{CQ}_\perp(M), \lesssim) \to (\mathrm{Tab}(G), \leq)$ has a dual adjoint $\mathrm{info}_\Delta : (\mathrm{Tab}(G), \leq) \to (\mathrm{CQ}_\perp(M), \lesssim)$, given by

$$\mathrm{info}_\Delta(T) := \begin{cases} (\Delta^T, \mathrm{col}_T) & \text{if } T \neq \emptyset \\ \mathsf{false} & \text{otherwise} \end{cases}, \tag{11}$$

where Δ^T is the *T-th power* of Δ (i.e. the T-fold direct product of Δ with itself) and $\mathrm{col}_T : \mathrm{schema}(T) \to G^T$ is the *column function* of T, i.e. $\mathrm{col}_T(x) := (t(x))_{t\in T}$ is the *x-column* of T. The query $\mathrm{info}_\Delta(T)$ is the most specific query (up to hom-equivalence) in $\mathrm{CQ}_\perp(M)$ that admits all rows of T as a solution; in that sense, it completely describes what the tuples in T have in common.

A *concept* of Δ is a pair $(T, Q) \in \mathrm{Tab}(G) \times \mathrm{CQ}_\perp(M)$ with $\mathrm{info}_\Delta(T) = Q$ and $\mathrm{res}_\Delta(Q) = T$. As usual, T is the *extent* and Q is the *intent* of (T, Q), and we simply write $T' := \mathrm{info}_\Delta(T)$ and $Q' := \mathrm{res}_\Delta(Q)$. The set of all concepts of Δ is denoted by $\mathcal{B}(\Delta)$. The *domain* of a concept $(T, Q) \in \mathcal{B}(\Delta)$ is the variable set $\mathrm{dom}(T, Q) := \mathrm{free}(Q) = \mathrm{schema}(T)$; the *bottom concept* $\perp := (\emptyset, \mathsf{false})$ has domain **var**, and the *top concept* $\top := (\{\langle\rangle\}, (\Delta, \langle\rangle))$ has domain $\emptyset$. The *X-slice* of $\mathcal{B}(\Delta)$, for a given $X \in \mathfrak{P}_{\mathrm{fin}}(\mathbf{var})$, is the complete sublattice $\mathcal{B}(\Delta)[X] := \{C \in \mathcal{B}(\Delta) \mid \mathrm{dom}(C) = X\} \cup \{\perp\}$. Infima and suprema of concepts are described by

$$(T_1, Q_1) \wedge (T_2, Q_2) = (T_1 \bowtie T_2, (Q_1 + Q_2)''), \tag{12}$$

$$(T_1, Q_1) \vee (T_2, Q_2) = ((T_1 \veebar T_2)'', Q_1 \times Q_2), \tag{13}$$

and likewise for families $(T_i, Q_i)_{i\in I}$ of concepts. The choice of the concept intent of a concept (T, Q) is somewhat arbitrary, because any other hom-equivalent

$R \simeq Q$ could be used as a representative. So for convenience, if $R \simeq Q$, we may say that (T, R) is a concept (and R is a concept intent), although strictly speaking, only (T, Q) with $Q = \text{info}_\Delta(T)$ is an element of $\mathcal{B}(\Delta)$. Note that, for practical purposes, the intents $\text{info}_\Delta(T) = (\Delta^T, \text{col}_T)$ in (11) can be simplified; it is sufficient to consider connected components of Δ^T, to which query minimization by folding can be applied [3][1, Sect. 6.2]; as an example, consider the second power $\mathcal{F}^2$ of the "family tree" $\mathcal{F}$ in [10, Figs. 5,1], and the representations of the intents in the slice $\mathcal{B}(\mathcal{F})[\{x\}]$ obtained from it [10, Fig. 2].

3   Orbital Concept Lattices

As can be inferred from (11), cf. [12, Prop. 15], the concept intents (except for false) are, up to hom-equivalence, precisely the queries (Δ^α, ν), where α is a cardinal and $\nu \in \text{NTup}(G^\alpha)$. This means, if we change the window of a concept intent, we obtain another concept intent. We now have a look at how this can be done systematically.

3.1   Finite Partial Transformations

A *finite partial transformation* on **var** is a function $\lambda \in \mathbf{var}^X$ defined on some $X \in \mathfrak{P}_{\text{fin}}(\mathbf{var})$. The set of finite partial transformations is denoted by $\mathcal{T}_{\text{fp}}(\mathbf{var})$. Note that formally $\mathcal{T}_{\text{fp}}(\mathbf{var}) = \text{NTup}(\mathbf{var})$; but a change of notation might be useful, to reflect the change of perspective. For $\lambda \in \mathbf{var}^X$, we call $\text{def}(\lambda) := X$ the *definition domain*, and $\text{rng}(\lambda) := \{\lambda(x) \mid x \in X\}$ the *range* of λ. Composition is defined for arbitrary $\lambda, \mu \in \mathcal{T}_{\text{fp}}(\mathbf{var})$ by $(\mu \circ \lambda)(x) := \mu(\lambda(x))$ for all $x \in \text{def}(\mu \circ \lambda) := \lambda_1^{-1}(\text{def}(\mu))$. Thus, the pair $(\mathcal{T}_{\text{fp}}(\mathbf{var}), \circ)$ is a semigroup.

3.2   Semigroup Actions

Accordingly, partial transformations can be composed with named tuples; we define $\circ : \text{NTup}(G) \times \mathcal{T}_{\text{fp}}(\mathbf{var}) \to \text{NTup}(G)$ by $(\nu \circ \lambda)(x) := (\nu(\lambda(x))$ for all $x \in \text{def}(\nu \circ \lambda) := \lambda^{-1}(\text{def}(\nu))$. We have $(\nu \circ \lambda_1) \circ \lambda_2 = \nu \circ (\lambda_1 \circ \lambda_2)$ for all $\nu \in \text{NTup}(G)$ and $\lambda_1, \lambda_2 \in \mathcal{T}_{\text{fp}}(\mathbf{var})$, i.e. composition is a (right) semigroup action; the semigroup $(\mathcal{T}_{\text{fp}}(\mathbf{var}), \circ)$ acts on $\text{NTup}(G)$. By extension, we obtain a semigroup action $\cdot : \text{CQ}_\perp(M) \times \mathcal{T}_{\text{fp}}(\mathbf{var}) \to \text{CQ}_\perp(M)$ on tableau queries, where

$$(\mathcal{G}, \nu) \cdot \lambda := (\mathcal{G}, \nu \circ \lambda), \tag{14}$$

$$\text{false} \cdot \lambda := \text{false}; \tag{15}$$

and a semigroup action $\cdot : \text{Tab}(G) \times \mathcal{T}_{\text{fp}}(\mathbf{var}) \to \text{Tab}(G)$ on tables, defined by

$$T \cdot \lambda := \{t \circ \lambda \mid t \in T\}. \tag{16}$$

So, since $\text{res}_\Delta(\mathcal{G}, \nu \circ \lambda) = \text{Hom}(\mathcal{G}, \Delta) \circ \nu \circ \lambda = \text{res}_\Delta(\mathcal{G}, \nu) \cdot \lambda$, we have

$$\text{res}_\Delta(Q \cdot \lambda) = \text{res}_\Delta(Q) \cdot \lambda \tag{17}$$

for all $Q \in \mathrm{CQ}_\perp(M)$; for $Q = \mathsf{false}$, we verify this separately. In other words: The change on a query's window is mirrored by a change of the result table. This means that the semigroup action can be extended to concepts: if (T, Q) is a concept, then $Q \cdot \lambda$ is a concept intent (as observed initially), and $T \cdot \lambda$ is the corresponding extent; i.e. the multiplication $\cdot : \mathcal{B}(\Delta) \times \mathcal{T}_{\mathrm{fp}}(\mathbf{var}) \to \mathcal{B}(\Delta)$ with

$$(T, Q) \cdot \lambda := (T \cdot \lambda, Q \cdot \lambda) \qquad (18)$$

is well-defined. Before we study in detail what multiplication with λ means, some more notation shall be introduced.

3.3   More Notation for Finite Partial Transformations

First, while the functions in $\mathcal{T}_{\mathrm{fp}}(\mathbf{var})$ are considered partial with respect to composition, it is convenient, in other respects, to treat them like total functions. For example, we write $\lambda : X \to Y$ to state that $\mathrm{def}(\lambda) = X$ and $\mathrm{rng}(\lambda) \subseteq Y$, or $\lambda : X \twoheadrightarrow Y$ if $\mathrm{def}(\lambda) = X$ and $\mathrm{rng}(\lambda) = Y$. In the latter case (where Y is clear) we may call λ a *surjection*, or a *bijection* if λ is injective. For each $X \in \mathfrak{P}_{\mathrm{fin}}(\mathbf{var})$, the function $\pi_X : X \to \mathbf{var}$, given by $\pi_X(x) = x$ for all $x \in X$, is called a *local identity*. Every $\lambda \in \mathcal{T}_{\mathrm{fp}}(\mathbf{var})$ has a *right inverse* $\lambda^{-r} \in \mathcal{T}_{\mathrm{fp}}(\mathbf{var})$, i.e. a function $\lambda^{-r} : \mathrm{rng}(\lambda) \to \mathrm{def}(\lambda)$ such that $\lambda \circ \lambda^{-r} = \pi_{\mathrm{rng}(\lambda)}$ holds; we assume that λ^{-r} is some fixed right inverse. If λ is injective, then $\lambda^{-1} := \lambda^{-r}$ is its *inverse*.

For every $\lambda \in \mathcal{T}_{\mathrm{fp}}(\mathbf{var})$ and $X \in \mathfrak{P}_{\mathrm{fin}}(\mathbf{var})$, the *restriction* of λ to X is the function $\lambda|_X := \lambda \circ \pi_X$, so $\mathrm{def}(\lambda|_X) = \mathrm{def}(\lambda) \cap X$. The *astriction* of λ to X is $\lambda|^X := \pi_X \circ \lambda$. The astriction $\lambda|^X : \lambda^{-1}(X) \to X$ so defined is actually a restriction to $\lambda^{-1}(X)$. For $z_1, \ldots, z_n \in \mathbf{var}$ and distinct $y_1, \ldots, y_n \in \mathbf{var}$, the *modification* $\lambda \frac{z_1 \ldots z_n}{y_1 \ldots y_n}$ is defined by $\mathrm{def}(\lambda \frac{z_1 \ldots z_n}{y_1 \ldots y_n}) = \mathrm{def}(\lambda) \cup \{y_1, \ldots, y_n\}$ and

$$\lambda \tfrac{z_1 \ldots z_n}{y_1 \ldots y_n}(x) := \begin{cases} z_i & \text{if } x = y_i \quad (\text{for } i \in \{1, \ldots, n\}) \\ \lambda(x) & \text{otherwise} \end{cases} . \qquad (19)$$

In particular, we formally have $\pi_\emptyset \frac{z_1 \ldots z_n}{y_1 \ldots y_n} = \langle y_1{:}z_1, \ldots, y_n{:}z_n \rangle$, and by abuse of notation, simply write $\frac{z_1 \ldots z_n}{y_1 \ldots y_n}$.

3.4   Special Transformations

There are three cases of λ that have special significance (cf. Figs. 3 and 4):

Local Identity For each $X \in \mathfrak{P}_{\mathrm{fin}}(\mathbf{var})$, the *local identity* $\pi_X : X \to \mathbf{var}$ is defined by $\pi(x) := x$ for $x \in X$. On $\mathrm{Tab}(G)$ it acts as projection, i.e. the table $T \cdot \pi_X$ is the projection of T to the columns in $\mathrm{schema}(T) \cap X$. On $\mathrm{CQ}(M)$ it acts as existential quantification, in the sense that $(\mathcal{G}, \nu) \cdot \pi_X$ is obtained from $(\mathcal{G}, \nu)$ by "anonymizing" the free variables in $\mathrm{free}(\mathcal{G}, \nu) \setminus X$.

Injections An injection $\xi : X \twoheadrightarrow Y$ can be considered a *local bijection*. On a table $T \in \mathrm{Tab}[Y]$, an injection $\xi : X \twoheadrightarrow Y$ acts as a one-to-one renaming of columns (renaming column $\xi(x)$ to x). On a query $Q \in \mathrm{CQ}[Y]$, it acts as a one-to-one substitution of free variables (replacing $\xi(x)$ by x).

Idempotents A function $\delta \in \text{NTup}(\mathbf{var})$ is (an) *idempotent* if $\delta \circ \delta = \delta$. It follows that $\delta : X \twoheadrightarrow Y$ is idempotent if and only if $Y \subseteq X$ and $\delta|_Y = \pi_Y$. Thus, on a table $T \in \text{Tab}[Y]$, an idempotent $\delta : X \twoheadrightarrow Y$ acts as column duplication (copying column $\delta(x)$ into a new column x, for all $x \in X \setminus Y$). On a query $Q \in \text{CQ}(M)[Y]$, it duplicates free variables (which corresponds to adding, for all $x \in X \setminus Y$, an atomic equality $x{=}\delta(x)$ to the query; note that x is a new variable here, which does not occur freely in Q).

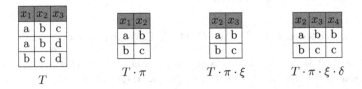

Fig. 3. Semigroup action with $\pi := \frac{x_1 x_2}{x_1 x_2}$, $\xi := \frac{x_1 x_2}{x_2 x_3}$, $\delta := \frac{x_2 x_3 x_3}{x_2 x_3 x_4}$

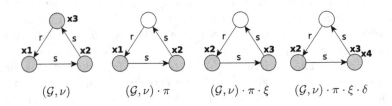

Fig. 4. Semigroup action with $\pi := \frac{x_1 x_2}{x_1 x_2}$, $\xi := \frac{x_1 x_2}{x_2 x_3}$, $\delta := \frac{x_2 x_3 x_3}{x_2 x_3 x_4}$

The following lemma helps to understand what multiplication with λ means:

Lemma 1 (Decomposition Lemma). *Every finite partial transformation $\lambda : Z \twoheadrightarrow X$ can be decomposed into a folding $\delta : Z \twoheadrightarrow Y_2$, a bijection $\xi : Y_2 \twoheadrightarrow Y_1$ and a partial identity $\pi : Y_1 \twoheadrightarrow X$, so that $\lambda = \pi \circ \xi \circ \delta$.*

Proof. A decomposition is $\lambda = \pi_{\text{rng}(\lambda)} \circ (\lambda^{-r})^{-1} \circ (\lambda^{-r} \circ \lambda)$. □

So e.g. if T is a table with schema X and $\lambda : Z \twoheadrightarrow X$, we obtain $T \cdot \lambda = T \cdot (\pi \circ \xi \circ \delta) = ((T \cdot \pi) \cdot \xi) \cdot \delta$, using a decomposition as in Lemma 1 and the semigroup action property; this means that multiplication with λ corresponds to a projection, a renaming, and a duplication operation, executed in that order. Multiplication with arbitrary $\lambda \in \mathcal{T}_{\text{fp}}(\mathbf{var})$ can be reduced the case $\lambda : Z \twoheadrightarrow X$, since $T \cdot \lambda = T \cdot \lambda|^X$ and $\lambda|^X : Z \twoheadrightarrow X$ for $Z := \lambda^{-1}(X)$. The same applies to the semigroup actions on named tuples, queries and concepts.

3.5   Star Queries

Now we formally introduce a special class of queries in $CQ_\perp(M)$, called star queries (cf. Fig. 2). An r-*star*, for a symbol $r \in M_n$, is a query $\mathcal{S}_r(y_1, \ldots, y_n) := ((\{a_1, \ldots, a_n\}, \mathfrak{a}), \langle y_1{:}a_1, \ldots, y_n{:}a_n \rangle)$, where $y_1, \ldots, y_n \in$ **var** are distinct variables, $a_1, \ldots, a_n$ are distinct nodes, $\mathfrak{a}(r) = \{(a_1, \ldots, a_n)\}$, and $\mathfrak{a}(m) = \emptyset$ for all $m \neq r$. A *star query* is an r-star, for some symbol r, or a query $\mathcal{E}(x, x)$. The following proposition will be illustrated by an example.

Proposition 1. *Every non-empty finite query can be built from star queries (up to isomorphism), using the operations $+, \cdot$ and the equality queries $\mathcal{E}(x, y)$.*

For an example, consider the query $(\mathcal{G}, \nu)$ in Fig. 1. The star queries in Fig. 2 constitute a decomposition of $(\mathcal{G}, \nu)$: each m-edge (for each $m \in M$) is represented by an m-star, and each isolated node by a query $\mathcal{E}(x, x)$; the free variables are chosen pairwise distinct, so that each star query is in its own connected component. We may understand Fig. 2 as depicting a single query Q_1 with four components, formally obtained by $Q_1 := \mathcal{E}(x_1, x_1) + \mathcal{S}_r(x_2, x_3, x_4, x_5) + \mathcal{S}_m(x_6) + \mathcal{S}_m(x_7)$. In a second step, we use equality queries to merge nodes, so that the structure of $\mathcal{G}$ is obtained; resulting in $Q_2 := Q_1 + \mathcal{E}(x_3, x_4) + \mathcal{E}(x_2, x_5) + \mathcal{E}(x_4, x_7) + \mathcal{E}(x_5, x_6)$; so up to isomorphism, we have $Q_2 = (\mathcal{G}, \langle x_1{:}c, x_2{:}a, x_3{:}b, x_4{:}b, x_5{:}a, x_6{:}a, x_7{:}b \rangle)$, and thus $(\mathcal{G}, \nu) = Q_2 \cdot \frac{x_6 x_1 x_1}{x_1 x_2 x_3}$.

3.6   Table Algebra and Concept Algebra

The *table algebra* over G, and the *concept algebra* over Δ, are defined by

$$\underline{\mathrm{Tab}}(G) := (\mathrm{Tab}(G), \bowtie, \emptyset, \{\langle\rangle\}, \cdot, (E_{xy})_{x,y \in \mathbf{var}}, \mathrm{schema}), \tag{20}$$

$$\underline{\mathcal{B}}(\Delta) := (\mathcal{B}(\Delta), \wedge, \perp, \top, \cdot, (\mathfrak{E}_{xy})_{x,y \in \mathbf{var}}, \mathrm{dom}), \tag{21}$$

respectively, where the concept $\mathfrak{E}_{xy} := (E_{xy}, (\mathcal{E}(x, y))'')$ is the *equality concept* for $x, y \in$ **var**.

4   Orbital Semilattices

The Basic Theorem on Concept Lattices [7, p.20] characterizes concept lattices as precisely (up to isomorphism) the complete lattices. In the previous section, we have equipped concept lattices with additional operations; with these operations come certain algebraic laws, that hold in every concept lattice $\mathcal{B}(\Delta)$; one may then ask, whether there is a finite set of axioms which characterize concept lattices of relational structures, in the style of a Basic Theorem.

In this paper, we present a partial solution, introducing orbital semilattices. We shall first verify the axioms for tables, then for concepts, and then explain their significance.

Definition 1 (Orbital Semilattice). *An* orbital semilattice *is an algebraic structure* $(V, \wedge, 0, 1, \cdot, (d_{xy})_{x,y \in \mathbf{var}}, \mathrm{dom})$ *consisting of an infimum operation* $\wedge$, *a bottom element* 0, *a top element* 1, *a right multiplication* $\cdot : V \times \mathcal{T}_{\mathrm{fp}}(\mathbf{var}) \to V$, *a diagonal* $d_{xy} \in V$ *for each* $(x, y) \in \mathbf{var} \times \mathbf{var}$, *and a domain function* $\mathrm{dom} : V \to \mathfrak{P}(\mathbf{var})$, *such that* $(V, \wedge, 0, 1)$ *is a bounded semilattice and the following axioms hold for all* $u, v \in V$, $\lambda, \mu \in \mathcal{T}_{\mathrm{fp}}(\mathbf{var})$, $x, y \in \mathbf{var}$ *and* $Y \in \mathfrak{P}_{\mathrm{fin}}(\mathbf{var})$.

(A1) $u \neq 0 \Rightarrow u \cdot \pi_\emptyset = 1$

(A2) $0 \cdot \lambda = 0$

(A3) $\mathrm{dom}(u) \subseteq Y$
$\Rightarrow (u \wedge v) \cdot \pi_Y = u \wedge v \cdot \pi_Y$

(A4) $u \leq u \cdot \pi_Y$

(A5) $u \leq v \Rightarrow u \cdot \lambda \leq v \cdot \lambda$

(A6) $(0 \neq u \leq d_{xy} \text{ and } x \neq y)$
$\Rightarrow u = (u \cdot \pi_{\mathrm{dom}(u) \setminus \{y\}}) \wedge d_{xy}$

(A7) $(u \cdot \lambda) \cdot \mu = u \cdot (\lambda \circ \mu)$

(A8) $u \cdot \pi_{\mathrm{dom}(u)} = u$

(A9) $d_{xx} \neq 0$

(A10) $d_{xy} = d_{xx} \cdot \frac{xx}{xy}$

(A11) $u \neq 0$
$\Rightarrow \mathrm{dom}(u \cdot \lambda) = \lambda^{-1}(\mathrm{dom}(u))$

(A12) $u \neq 0 \Rightarrow \mathrm{dom}(u)$ *is finite*

(A13) $\mathrm{dom}(u) = \{x \in \mathbf{var} \mid u \leq d_{xx}\}$

4.1 Example: Table Algebra

Theorem 1. *Let* $G \neq \emptyset$. *Then* $\underline{\mathrm{Tab}}(G)$ *is an orbital semilattice.*

Proof. Most axioms are straightforward to verify. For example, if $T \neq \emptyset$, then $T \cdot \pi_\emptyset = \{t \circ \pi_\emptyset \mid t \in T\} = \{\langle\rangle\}$ which shows **(A1)**. We only show **(A3)** and **(A6)**; the assumption $G \neq \emptyset$ is required for **(A9)**.

For proving **(A3)**, we assume $S \in \mathrm{Tab}(G)$ with $\mathrm{schema}(S) \subseteq Y$; then every $t \in S \bowtie (T \cdot \pi_Y)$ can be extended to a tuple $\tilde{t} \in S \bowtie T$, which means $t = \tilde{t} \circ \pi_Y \in (S \bowtie T) \cdot \pi_Y$; this shows $S \bowtie (T \cdot \pi_Y) \subseteq (S \bowtie T) \cdot \pi_Y$, and thus also $S \bowtie (T \cdot \pi_Y) \leq (S \bowtie T) \cdot \pi_Y$. The other inequality in **(A3)** derives from **(A5)**, **(A7)** and **(A8)** (which can be shown directly): since $\bowtie$ is the lattice infimum, we obtain $(S \bowtie T) \cdot \pi_Y \leq S \cdot \pi_Y \bowtie T \cdot \pi_Y$ using **(A5)**, moreover $S \cdot \pi_Y = S \cdot \pi_{\mathrm{schema}(S)} \cdot \pi_Y = S \cdot \pi_{\mathrm{schema}(S)} = S$ using **(A8)**, **(A7)** and $\mathrm{schema}(S) \subseteq Y$.

Axiom **(A6)** may look involved, but is essentially simple: It states that, if T is a table, and two table columns x and y are copies of each other (i.e. $t(x) = t(y)$ for all $t \in T$), then deleting the y-column (by projecting on the others), followed by duplicating x into y (by joining with E_{xy}) gives back the original table T. The condition $0 \neq u$ in **(A6)** ensures that $\pi_{\mathrm{dom}(u) \setminus \{y\}}$ is well-defined. $\qquad \square$

4.2 Subalgebras

A *subalgebra* of an orbital semilattice $(V, \wedge, 0, 1, \cdot, (d_{xy})_{x,y \in \mathbf{var}}, \mathrm{dom})$ is an algebra $(U, \wedge_U, 0, 1, \cdot_U, (d_{xy})_{x,y \in \mathbf{var}}, \mathrm{dom}_U)$ where $U \subseteq V$ is closed under $\wedge$ and $\cdot$, contains 0, 1 and d_{xy} for all $x, y \in \mathbf{var}$, and $\wedge_U$, $\cdot_U$ and dom_U denote the corresponding restrictions. Note that the implicit order $\leq_U$ on the subalgebra coincides with the order on V, i.e. $u \leq_U v \Leftrightarrow u = u \wedge_U v \Leftrightarrow u = u \wedge v \Leftrightarrow u \leq v$ for all $u, v \in U$. It is thus simple to check, using Def. 1, that subalgebras of orbital semilattices are again orbital semilattices.

Corollary 1. *Let* $G \neq \emptyset$. *Every subalgebra of* $\underline{\mathrm{Tab}}(G)$ *is an orbital semilattice.*

4.3   SPJR Algebra with Equalities

The SPJR algebra [1] consists of the operations (s)election, (p)rojection, natural (j)oin and (r)enaming. For any given $x, y \in$ **var**, the selection operation $\sigma_{x=y}$ is defined by $\sigma_{x=y}(T) := \{t \in T \mid t(x) = t(y)\}$ on any table T with $x, y \in$ schema(T). Abiteboul et al. [1, p. 57] also define a second kind of selection, which compares with a constant; since we do not allow constants in M (except as unary relation symbols, cf. Sect. 2.5), we assume selections are of the first kind only. The operations $\bowtie$ and $\cdot$ in $\underline{\text{Tab}}(G)$ provide almost the same set of operations (cf. Sect. 3.4) that we shall refer to as DPJR: (d)uplication, (p)rojection, natural (j)oin and (r)enaming.

If equalities E_{xy} are available, both sets of operations are equivalent, because both selection and duplication can then be expressed with the natural join: for $x, y \in$ schema(T), we have $\sigma_{x=y}(T) = T \bowtie E_{xy}$, and for an idempotent $\delta : Y \twoheadrightarrow$ schema(T) we have $T \cdot \delta = T \bowtie E_{y_1 \delta(y_1)} \bowtie \cdots \bowtie E_{y_n \delta(y_n)}$, where $y_1, \ldots, y_n$ are the elements of $Y \setminus$ schema(T).

This means that the subalgebra of $\underline{\text{Tab}}(G)$, generated from a set $U \subseteq \text{Tab}(G)$ and the special tables $\emptyset$, $\{\langle\rangle\}$ and E_{xy}, $x, y \in$ **var**, is the same with respect to both SPJR and DPJR. A formal advantage of using the set $\{\bowtie, \cdot\}$ of operations may be that both operations are total, whereas the other operations are typically considered to be partial operations.

4.4   Embedding of the Concept Algebra in the Table Algebra

Homomorphisms are defined in the obvious way, preserving all constants, operations and the domain. As usual for algebras, an *embedding* is an injective homomorphism. The function ext : $\mathcal{B}(\Delta) \rightarrow \text{Tab}(G)$, which maps each concept to its extent, is an embedding: it is injective, and from the definitions in Sect. 2.6, we obtain schema$(\text{ext}(C)) = \text{dom}(C)$, ext$(\bot) = \emptyset$ and ext$(\top) = \{\langle\rangle\}$; ext$(C_1 \wedge C_2) = \text{ext}(C_1) \bowtie \text{ext}(C_2)$ from (12), and ext$(C \cdot \lambda) = \text{ext}(C) \cdot \lambda$ from (18); and finally, ext$(\mathfrak{E}_{xy}) = E_{xy}$ by the definition in Sect. 3.6. Therefore, $\underline{\mathcal{B}}(\Delta)$ is isomorphic to a subalgebra of $\underline{\text{Tab}}(G)$, and Cor. 1 provides another corollary.

Corollary 2. *The concept algebra $\underline{\mathcal{B}}(\Delta)$ is an orbital semilattice if $|\Delta| \neq \emptyset$.*

4.5   The Subalgebra of Concepts Generated by Finite Queries

The set $\mathcal{B}_{\text{fin}}(\Delta) := \{(Q', Q'') \mid Q \text{ finite}\} \cup \{\bot\}$ contains the concepts that are generated by finite queries (plus the bottom concept). It forms a subalgebra $\underline{\mathcal{B}}_{\text{fin}}(\Delta)$ of $\underline{\mathcal{B}}(\Delta)$, cf. (12) and (18), and is thus an orbital semilattice:

Corollary 3. *The subalgebra $\underline{\mathcal{B}}_{\text{fin}}(\Delta)$ is an orbital semilattice if $|\Delta| \neq \emptyset$.*

5   Representation Theorem

The following theorem is shown in [13]. In fact, the whole paper consists of a single proof, showing that theorem (so it is too long to be included here). The significance for FCA is shown in the corollary below.

Theorem 2. *Every orbital semilattice V can be embedded in a table algebra* $\underline{\mathrm{Tab}}(G)$ *for some* $G \neq \emptyset$.

Corollary 4. *Every orbital semilattice V is isomorphic to a concept subalgebra* $\mathcal{B}_{\mathrm{fin}}(\Delta)$ *for some non-empty* Δ.

Proof. Theorem. 2 states that V is isomorphic to a subalgebra U of $\underline{\mathrm{Tab}}(G)$ for some non-empty G. We will define Δ such that the extents of $\mathcal{B}_{\mathrm{fin}}(\Delta)$ are precisely the elements of U; then $\mathcal{B}_{\mathrm{fin}}(\Delta)$ is isomorphic to U, and thus to V.

Let M be the relational signature given by $M_n := \{T \in U \mid \mathrm{schema}(T) = \{x_1, \ldots, x_n\}\}$ for all $n \geq 1$, and let Δ be the M-structure given by $|\Delta| := G$ and $T^{\Delta} := \{(g_1, \ldots, g_n) \mid \langle x_1{:}g_1, \ldots, x_n{:}g_n \rangle \in T\}$ for all $T \in M_n$ and $n \geq 1$. For each T-star (cf. Sect. 3.5), we have $\mathcal{S}_T(y_1, \ldots, y_n) = \mathcal{S}_T(x_1, \ldots, x_n) \cdot \frac{x_1 \ldots x_n}{y_1 \ldots y_n}$, so

$$\mathrm{res}_\Delta(\mathcal{S}_T(y_1, \ldots, y_n)) = T \cdot \frac{x_1 \ldots x_n}{y_1 \ldots y_n} \tag{22}$$

by (17) and the definition of Δ. In particular, $\mathrm{res}_\Delta(\mathcal{S}_T(y_1, \ldots, y_n)) \in U$. Also, $\mathrm{res}_\Delta(\mathcal{E}(x, y)) = E_{xy} \in U$. By Prop. 1, every non-empty finite query Q is built from these basic queries using $+$ and $\cdot$, which res_Δ preserves by (10) and (17), i.e. $\mathrm{res}_\Delta(Q) \in U$. In addition, $\mathrm{res}_\Delta(\mathsf{true}) = \{\langle\rangle\} \in U$ and $\mathrm{res}_\Delta(\mathsf{false}) = \emptyset \in U$, which shows that all extents of $\mathcal{B}_{\mathrm{fin}}(\Delta)$ are tables in U.

Conversely, a table $T \in U \setminus \{\emptyset, \{\langle\rangle\}\}$ has schema $\{y_1, \ldots, y_n\}$ for some $n \geq 1$, and for $\xi := \frac{y_1 \ldots y_n}{x_1 \ldots x_n}$ we have $T \cdot \xi \in M_n$ and $\mathrm{res}_\Delta(\mathcal{S}_{T \cdot \xi}(y_1, \ldots, y_n)) = (T \cdot \xi) \cdot \xi^{-1} = T$ by (22), (**A7**) and (**A8**), so T is an extent in $\mathcal{B}_{\mathrm{fin}}(\Delta)$. The same holds for $T = \{\langle\rangle\}$ and $T = \emptyset$; so every table in U is also an extent in $\mathcal{B}_{\mathrm{fin}}(\Delta)$.   □

6   Related Work

Concept lattices of relational structures have been introduced in [10], and the connection to database theory was further elaborated in [12, Sects. 3,4]. The concept lattice $\mathcal{B}(\Delta)$ corresponds to the lattice $\mathfrak{L}_D$ (not $\mathfrak{C}_D$) in [10]. The lattice $\mathfrak{L}_D$ in that paper is a variant of $\mathcal{B}(\Delta)$ which provides for tables with infinite headers (i.e. it contains slices $\mathfrak{L}_D[X]$ for infinite $X \subseteq \mathbf{var}$); moreover, tables with explicit headers have been used; the difference is that there is a separate empty table for every schema X. With implicit headers, there is only a single empty table, which allows the set representation pset : $\mathrm{Tab}(G) \to \mathfrak{P}(\mathrm{NTup}(G))$ of tables (cf. Sect 2.2), so that concept lattices of relational structures are formally obtained as a special case of pattern structures [6][12, Sect. 6].

Imieliński and Lipski [9] describe a similar embedding $h : \mathrm{Tab}(G) \to \mathfrak{P}(G^{\mathbf{var}})$, but require conditions [9, Thm. 2] that amount to tables being finite and G being infinite; whereas pset is always an embedding. The conditions stem from the fact that h is geared toward the usual predicate logical semantics, identifying tables with sets in a cylindric set algebra [9] [8]. The orbital semilattices of this paper have many commonalities with cylindric algebras, but they are semilattices only, without a complement operation; the diagonals are present, but the axiom $d_{xx} = 1$ of cylindric algebras (cf. [8]) is not satisfied; the domain corresponds to the dimension set, but axiom **(A13)** does not work for cylindric algebras (since $d_{xx} = 1$); in future work, the semigroup action will be reduced to cylindrification; this will enable a better comparison.

On the other hand, the semigroup action is a key element in the proof of Thm. 2 [13]. Moreover, it introduces a notion of orbits on concept lattices of relational structures; this provides a connection to concept lattice orbifolds[1], introduced by Borchmann and Ganter [2]. The connection is as follows: The semigroup action on $\mathcal{B}(\Delta)$ induces a preorder on the concepts, defined by $C_1 \sqsubseteq C_2 :\Leftrightarrow \exists \lambda \in \mathcal{T}_{\mathrm{fp}}(\mathbf{var}) : C_1 \cdot \lambda = C_2$, where reflexivity and symmetry follow from **(A8)** and **(A7)**; the orbits are the equivalence classes w.r.t. the preorder; this generalizes the notion of orbits (conventionally defined for group actions). The intuition is that a projection π_X casts a concept into a higher orbit, whereas local bijections ξ or idempotents δ (cf. Sect 3.4) preserve the orbits. A group of local bijections $\xi : X \twoheadrightarrow X$, acting on a slice $\mathcal{B}(\Delta)[X]$, induces an orbifold in the sense of Borchmann and Ganter. This connection could be further investigated.

The projection of concepts has been first described by Ferré [4,5]. Otherwise, the development in [4] largely mirrors that in [10], although a different formalism is used, without the tables and join that connect concepts to relational algebra.

Since $(\mathrm{Tab}(G), \leq)$ is a complete lattice, the natural join (which represents the infimum) is accompanied by a supremum operation, which is called the *co-join* in [10], and denoted by x. The lattice of tables, with the join and co-join operations, was previously described by Spight and Tropashko [15], who call the co-join an *inner union* but use the same symbol x. The lattice has been called a *relational lattice* [15] or *Tropashko lattice* [14]; the latter paper writes $\oplus$ for the inner union. Litak et al. [14] investigate Tropashko lattices, also in terms of axiomatizability; however, orbital semilattices, by Thm. 2, are generally not Tropashko lattices, but subsemilattices thereof. The tables in [14] have explicit headers, and as Litak et al. show, this allows a clever encoding of our domain function dom : $V \to \mathfrak{P}_{\mathrm{fin}}(\mathbf{var})$ by a single *header constant* H. Interestingly, Litak et al. use FCA to study arrow relations of Tropashko lattices.

7 Conclusion

The connection between FCA and database theory has been further enhanced by the introduction of orbital concept lattices, which combine the extensional viewpoint of SPJR algebra with equality, and the intensional viewpoint of conjunctive calculus with equality, as embodied by the semilattice operation which is the natural extension of concept lattices of relational structures to this sort of expressivity. While equality queries and tables are rather untypical assumptions with regard to Codd's relational data model, we could say (from an opposite viewpoint) that the paper exemplifies, taking a middle ground between database theory and logic, that relational algebra and conjunctive queries are (albeit conventionally) not necessarily tied to Codd's model (cf. Sect. 2.5, first paragraph). There is arguably as much overlap with algebraic logic as there is with database

---

[1] Thanks to one of the anonymous reviewers for the insightful remark.

theory, although the work seems to fit neither of the two categories perfectly. But there is some ongoing research focusing on the connection of the two (cf. [14]) and maybe this could be where such kind of research fits. In any case, the main motivation lies on the further development of concept lattices of relational structures, and the main result of this paper, namely that orbital semilattices are precisely the subalgebras $\underline{\mathcal{B}}_{\text{fin}}(\Delta)$, is a nontrivial result that is likely a major step towards a Basic Theorem (cf. Sect. 4, first paragraph) for concept lattices of relational structures.

References

1. Abiteboul, S., Hull, R., Vianu, V.: Foundations of Databases. Addison-Wesley, Boston (1995)
2. Borchmann, D., Ganter, B.: Concept lattice orbifolds – first steps. In: Ferré, S., Rudolph, S. (eds.) ICFCA 2009. LNCS (LNAI), vol. 5548, pp. 22–37. Springer, Heidelberg (2009). https://doi.org/10.1007/978-3-642-01815-2_2
3. Chandra, A.K., Merlin, P.M.: Optimal implementation of conjunctive queries in relational databases. In: Proceedings of the Ninth Annual ACM Symposium on Theory of Computing, STOC '77, pp. 77–90. ACM, New York, NY, USA (1977)
4. Ferré, S.: A proposal for extending formal concept analysis to knowledge graphs. In: Baixeries, J., Sacarea, C., Ojeda-Aciego, M. (eds.) ICFCA 2015. LNCS (LNAI), vol. 9113, pp. 271–286. Springer, Cham (2015). https://doi.org/10.1007/978-3-319-19545-2_17
5. Ferré, S., Cellier, P.: Graph-FCA: an extension of formal concept analysis to knowledge graphs. Discret. Appl. Math. **273**, 81–102 (2020)
6. Ganter, B., Kuznetsov, S.O.: Pattern structures and their projections. In: Delugach, H.S., Stumme, G. (eds.) ICCS-ConceptStruct 2001. LNCS (LNAI), vol. 2120, pp. 129–142. Springer, Heidelberg (2001). https://doi.org/10.1007/3-540-44583-8_10
7. Ganter, B., Wille, R.: Formal Concept Analysis: Mathematical Foundations. Springer, Heidelberg (1999). https://doi.org/10.1007/978-3-642-59830-2
8. Henkin, L., Monk, J.D., Tarski, A.: Cylindric Algebras, Part 1. North-Holland, Amsterdam (1971)
9. Imieliński, T., Lipski, W.: The relational model of data and cylindric algebras. J. Comput. Syst. Sci. **28**(1), 80–102 (1984)
10. Kötters, J.: Concept lattices of a relational structure. In: Pfeiffer, H.D., Ignatov, D.I., Poelmans, J., Gadiraju, N. (eds.) ICCS-ConceptStruct 2013. LNCS (LNAI), vol. 7735, pp. 301–310. Springer, Heidelberg (2013). https://doi.org/10.1007/978-3-642-35786-2_23
11. Kötters, J., Eklund, P.W.: The theory and practice of coupling formal concept analysis to relational databases. In: Kuznetsov, S.O., Napoli, A., Rudolph, S. (eds.) Proceedings of FCA4AI 2018. CEUR Workshop Proceedings, vol. 2149, pp. 69–80. CEUR-WS.org (2018)
12. Kötters, J., Eklund, P.W.: Conjunctive query pattern structures: a relational database model for formal concept analysis. Discret. Appl. Math. **273**, 144–171 (2020)
13. Kötters, J., Schmidt, S.E.: Orbital semilattices (2022). https://arxiv.org/abs/2206.07790

14. Litak, T., Mikulás, S., Hidders, J.: Relational lattices: from databases to universal algebra. JLAMP **85**(4), 540–573 (2016)
15. Spight, M., Tropashko, V.: First steps in relational lattice (2006). https://arxiv.org/abs/cs/0603044

Semiotic Conceptual Analysis of Part-Whole Relationships in Diagrams

Uta Priss[(⊠)]

Fakultät Informatik, Ostfalia University, Wolfenbüttel, Germany
u.priss@ostfalia.de
http://www.upriss.org.uk

Abstract. Proverbially, a picture is worth a 1000 words because it conveys a multitude of concepts, their parts and relationships simultaneously. But it is difficult to precisely describe why and how a picture achieves this. This paper employs Semiotic Conceptual Analysis as a means for providing formal methods for analysing diagrams and other graphical representations, in particular, by modelling part-whole relationships amongst representations and defining quantitative measures and certain qualitative features for comparing different types of representations. The general background for this research is analysing diagrams for teaching purposes.

1 Introduction

A background for this research is mathematics education research. Mathematical concepts often involve several types of representations many of which are diagrammatic. It is well known that mathematical content should be taught using "multiple representations" (Ainsworth 1999). For example, a function can be represented in different formats (as a set, relation, graph, piece of computer code and so on) and using different media (with pen and paper or with a variety of computational tools). Expert mathematicians use and switch between different representations seamlessly often without even being aware of it. But students need to learn when and how to employ representations and how to integrate them into joined-up concepts. For a mathematics teacher the questions arise as to which representations are most effective, how many different types should be used, in which order they should be introduced and so on. While many publications on graphs and diagrams already exist (e.g. Moody (2009)), there is still a need for a development of algorithmic, structural approaches. In this paper we are proposing to use Semiotic Conceptual Analysis (SCA) as a method for analysing and comparing diagrams and other graphical representations. A future goal is to develop computerised tools that support teachers in their decision processes of selecting and structuring teaching materials.

SCA is a formalisation of semiotics based on modelling signs as elements of a triadic relation (Priss 2017). SCA was initially influenced by the semiotics of Charles S. Peirce but its purpose is not philosophy. Instead, SCA can be considered an extension of Formal Concept Analysis (FCA) which is a formalisation of concept hierarchies (Ganter and Wille 1999). Both SCA and FCA are mathematical approaches to modelling data.

T. Braun et al. (Eds.): ICCS 2022, LNCS 13403, pp. 82–96, 2022.
https://doi.org/10.1007/978-3-031-16663-1_7

Therefore signs as defined by SCA and concepts as defined by FCA are abstractions of their philosophical or linguistic counterparts. Once data has been modelled by a user according to SCA or FCA, signs or concepts are deterministically identified by their structural properties. Diagrams and other graphical representations tend to contain parts and are therefore compound signs in SCA. A text containing words which themselves contain letters is also an example of a compound sign. This paper presents a semiotic approach for comparing compound signs, their parts and relationships which applies to many different types of representations without defining grammars or other domain-specific structures. Some of the notions were already introduced in Priss (2022) but are further extended in this paper. All propositions and examples in this paper are new. SCA has previously been applied in a variety of settings (Priss 2019) and has established a vocabulary pertaining to different semiotic topics.

There are other existing theories which consider how semiotic structures are trans-mitted (e.g. Information Theory) or transformed, such as representation theory, Barwise and Seligman's (1997) information flow theory, Goguen's (1999) algebraic semiotics, theories of formal languages and grammars and others. But such theories tend to focus on proving properties of classes of structures or on certain types of problems. The aim of SCA, however, is to provide means for analysing finite data collected from actual appli-cations. Furthermore, other existing theories tend to use sets as their smallest building blocks in contrast to the use of triadic signs in SCA. Last but not least, there are many methods for analysing graphical representations (e.g. Moody 2009) but they do not tend to build coherent mathematical theories. Questions about diagrams could also be answered by conducting user studies. But that would be a more time consuming app-roach than a structural analysis with SCA.

Apart from being influenced by Peirce's philosophy, another motivation for SCA was to improve concept lattices developed for natural language data such as the lattices generated from WordNet and Roget's Thesaurus by Priss and Old (2010). The struc-tures emerging from words and their meanings do not automatically resemble intuitive conceptual hierarchies or maintain part-whole relationships because of synonymy and polysemy amongst words and because the relationships within the data are normally created in a somewhat ad-hoc manner. Signs are triadic instead of binary. Thus a semi-otic relation can be considered a formal context (in the sense of FCA) where each "cross" is replaced by a set of partial functions that determine under which conditions a cross is relevant. From the view of Triadic FCA, similar contexts are discussed by Ganter and Obiedkov (2004).

The following section repeats SCA core notions and ensures that this paper is self-contained with respect to SCA. Because FCA has been presented many times before at this conference, it is assumed that readers are familiar with FCA. Section 3 describes how compound representamens can be decomposed in a manner that provides measur-able features. Sections 4 and 5 apply the theory developed in this paper to two examples of mathematical representations which present typical topics taught in undergraduate mathematics. The paper finishes with a conclusion.

2   Basic SCA Notions

While an FCA *concept* is a pair of a set called *extension* and a set called *intension*, a *sign* in SCA is a triple whose three elements are called *interpretation, representamen* and *denotation*. There are no further restrictions placed on the sets of representamens and denotations. But the interpretations must be partial functions from the set of representamens into the set of denotations which means that if an interpretation is defined for a representamen then it must map the representamen onto a unique denotation. If SCA is applied to linguistic data then representamens might be words or lexemes, denotations might be word or lexeme meanings and interpretations might be usage contexts. A set of signs with shared sets of interpretations, representamens and denotations is called a *semiotic relation*. If SCA is applied to diagrams, a user first identifies interpretations that are relevant. Usually different interpretations are applied simultaneously to different parts of a diagram yielding a complex conceptual structure which is then further analysed with SCA and FCA. Compound signs which are defined more precisely below have a denotation as a whole but also denotations via their parts.

Figure 1 displays an example of a tiny semiotic relation with 4 signs. The sign s_1 has '15' as its representamen, '15 minutes' as its denotation and $i_1('15') =$ '15 minutes' using some interpretation i_1. In this example the representamens and denotations are strings, but representamens can also be pictures and denotations can be concepts from an FCA concept lattice. Representamens are usually specified based on an equivalence relation. In Fig. 1, 'quarter' and 'QUARTER' might be considered equivalent for an SCA analysis. According to the following definition, the only requirement for these 4 triples is that their interpretations must be partial functions which means that s_2 and s_3 must use different interpretations.

$$s_1 = (i_1, \text{'15', '15 minutes'})$$
$$s_2 = (i_1, \text{'quarter', '25 cents'})$$
$$s_3 = (i_2, \text{'QUARTER', '15 minutes'})$$
$$s_4 = (i_2, \text{'25', 'a natural number with value 25'})$$

Fig. 1. Example of a tiny semiotic relation with 4 signs

is not explicitly represented. Different decompositions can exist for a representamen. For instance, the representamen 74 can also be decomposed into a '7' interpreted as a decimal position and a '4' in a unary position. As a Roman numeral, LXXIV contains 5 parts, 4 of which are added and one is subtracted. The numeral X occurs twice with the same interpretation.

Proposition 1. *For* $(R, \leq)$ *with a decomposition* $\phi \in \Phi$:

a) $(r \in R_\phi$ *and* $r < r_1) \Longleftrightarrow r \in \phi(r_1)_{|R}$
b) $\phi(r_1)_{|R} \subseteq R_\phi$
c) $r_1 = r_2 \Longrightarrow \phi(r_1) = \phi(r_2)$
d) $r_1 \leq r_2 \Longrightarrow \phi(r_1)_{|R} \subseteq \phi(r_2)_{|R}$

Proof: a) and b) follow from Definition 4. c) is true because ϕ is a function. d) follows from a) because $r \in \phi(r_1)_{|R} \Longrightarrow r < r_1 \Longrightarrow r < r_2$ and $r < r_2 \Longrightarrow r \in \phi(r_2)_{|R}$.

Proposition 1c) and d) only apply if the same R_ϕ is involved. For example, in Table 1, $(3,5)< \{(3,5),(4,6)\}$ and $\phi_g((3,5)) \subseteq \phi_g(\{(3,5),(4,6)\})$ but $\phi_g((3,5)) \not\subseteq \phi_{g1}(\{(3,5),(4,6)\})$. Definition 4 does not force a representamen to always be used with the same interpretation or that representamens are physically non-overlapping.

One might distinguish *positional* decompositions and interpretations which describe the exact or relative position of parts within compounds, for example using coordinates, and *grammatical* decompositions and interpretations which determine some type or category for each representamen. For images, a bitmap decomposes an image positionally by providing locations (as interpretations) for each colour pixel (as representamens). A grammatical decomposition of an image is a vector graphical representation. In Table 1, interpretations indexed with p... and decomposition ϕ_p are positional. Both grammatical and positional decompositions may contain an interpretation i_m which indicates punctuation marks. A part together with a grammatical interpretation tends to generate a sign that is useful even outside the context of a compound, parts with positional interpretations usually do not. For example, a sign for '70' (extracted from '74') might be useful, but a sign for '7 in the decimal position' is probably not of interest. The next definition discusses how to reconstruct a partial order amongst representamens from decompositions.

Table 1. Examples of decompositions (representamens in bold without quotes)

$\phi_g(\mathbf{74}) = \{(i_{d10},7), (i_{d1},4)\}$
$\phi_p(\mathbf{74}) = \{(i_{p1},7), (i_{p2},4)\}$
$\phi_g(\mathbf{LXXIV}) = \{(i_{add},L), (i_{add},X), (i_{add},X)_1, (i_{sub},I), (i_{add},V)\}$
$\phi_p(\mathbf{LXXIV}) = \{(i_{p1},L), (i_{p2},X), (i_{p3},X), (i_{p4},I), (i_{p5},V)\}$
$\phi_g(\{\mathbf{(3,5),(4,6)}\}) = \{(i_{le},3), (i_{ri},5), (i_{le},4), (i_{ri},6), (i_m, \{), (i_m,(), (i_m,()_1, (i_m,,),$
         $(i_m,,)_1, (i_m,,)_2, (i_m,)), (i_m,))_1, (i_m, \})\}$
$\phi_p(\{\mathbf{(3,5),(4,6)}\}) = \{(i_{p1.1},3), (i_{p1.2},5), (i_{p2.1},4), (i_{p2.2},6), (i_m, \{), (i_m,(), ...(i_m, \})\}$
$\phi_{g1}(\{\mathbf{(3,5),(4,6)}\}) = \{(i_e,\mathbf{(3,5)}), (i_e,\mathbf{(4,6)}), (i_m, \{), (i_m, \}), (i_m,,)\}$
$\phi_g(\mathbf{(3,5)}) = \{(i_{le},3), (i_{ri},5), (i_m,(), (i_m,,), (i_m,))\}$
with $R_{\phi_g} = R_{\phi_p} = \{1, 2, ..., 9, I, V, X, L, C, \{, \}, (,), ...\}$ and $R_{\phi_{g1}} = \{(1, 1), (1, 2), ...\{, \}, ...\}$

88   U. Priss

Definition 5. *For $(R, \leq)$ with a set Φ of decompositions, $\phi \in \Phi$ is called* reversible *if for all $r_1, r_2 \in R$ with non-empty $\phi(r_1)$, $r_1 \leq r_2 \iff \phi(r_1) \subseteq \phi(r_2)$.*
A set $\Phi_1 \subseteq \Phi$ is called reversible *if for all $r_1, r_2 \in R$ the following two conditions hold:*
$(\phi(r_1) \neq \emptyset$ *for all* $\phi \in \Phi_1) \implies (r_1 \leq r_2 \iff (\forall \phi_m \in \Phi_1)\, \phi_m(r_1) \subseteq \phi_m(r_2))$,
$(\exists \phi \in \Phi_1$ *with* $\phi(r_1) = \emptyset) \implies (r_1 \leq r_2 \iff (\exists \phi_n \in \Phi_1)\, r_1 \in \phi_n(r_2)_{|R})$.
Analogous definitions apply to a reversible $\phi_\star$ and a reversible $\Phi_{\star 1}$.

The condition involving ϕ_m means that all ϕ_m must agree in order for $r_1 \leq r_2$ to hold. The condition involving ϕ_n builds on Proposition 1a. A reversible ϕ ensures that some upper part of $(R, \leq)$, a reversible Φ_1 that the complete $(R, \leq)$ can be constructed from the decompositions. For Table 1, $\phi_g((3,5)) \subseteq \phi_g(\{(3,5),(4,6)\})$ but also $\phi_g((3,6)) \subseteq \phi_g(\{(3,5),(4,6)\})$. Therefore, ϕ_g is not reversible and by itself insufficient to determine $(R, \leq)$. But $\Phi_1 = \{g, g1\}$ is a reversible set of decompositions because $\phi_{g1}((3,6)) = \emptyset$ and only $(3,5) \in \phi_{g1}(\{(3,5),(4,6)\})_{|R}$. As another example, a decomposition of a text into letters is not reversible but in combination with further decompositions corresponding to parse trees (words, parts of sentences, paragraphs and so on) a set of decompositions could be reversible. Restoring a representamen from its parts (if ϕ is bijective) also requires some rules with respect to how the parts fit together. SCA assumes that such rules are stored somewhere but they are not discussed explicitly by SCA. The rules for restoring from a bijective positional decomposition tend to be simpler than from a grammatical decomposition. Grammatical interpretations also provide positional information but in a less deterministic manner. For example, i_{sub} states that a Roman numeral is to the left of the next larger numeral but if several 'X's occur, their order is not determined (and not relevant). For natural languages some grammatical categories determine locations (such as subject-predicate-object in English) but some are flexible. Thus both positional and grammatical interpretations have some advantages and disadvantages.

Proposition 2. *If ϕ is reversible and $\phi(r_1) \neq \emptyset$, then $r_1 = r_2 \iff \phi(r_1) = \phi(r_2)$*

Proof: '$\implies$' because ϕ is a function. '$\impliedby$' $\phi(r_1) = \phi(r_2) \implies \phi(r_1) \subseteq \phi(r_2)$ and $\phi(r_2) \subseteq \phi(r_1) \implies r_1 \leq r_2$ and $r_2 \leq r_1$.

Thus a reversible ϕ means that the parts contain sufficient information to identify a compound. Each Φ generates a formal context as described in the next definition, but contexts use sets instead of multisets.

Definition 6. *For $(R, \leq)$ with a set Φ of decompositions, a* decomposition context *is a formal context $(\bigcup_{\phi,r} \phi_\star(r), R, J)$ with $(i_1, r_1)Jr_2 \iff r_1 = r_2$ or $(\exists \phi_\star \in \Phi_\star)$ $(i_1, r_1) \in \phi_\star(r_2)$. The corresponding lattices are called* decomposition lattices.

Figure 2 shows an example of a decomposition lattice for ϕ_g from Table 1. In this case, the lattice order preserves the partial order amongst representamens. But that would not be the case if a representamen $(3,6)$ was added because ϕ_g is not reversible.

A non-reversible ϕ will lose some information about representamens. Furthermore because lattices are constructed using sets they omit information about multiple occurrences of parts. Therefore in general, a decomposition lattice generates its own partial order amongst representamens which need not correspond to $(R, \leq)$. It is therefore of

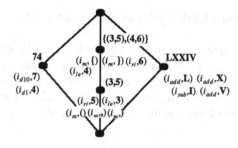

Fig. 2. A decomposition lattice for ϕ_g from Table 1

interest to specify under which conditions $(R, \leq)$ is maintained in a decomposition lattice.

Proposition 3. *For $(R, \leq)$ with a reversible $\phi_* \in \Phi$ and $(\bigcup_r \phi_*(r), R, J)$ as a decomposition context, it follows that $(\forall r \in R) \ r' = \phi_*(r)$ and $r_1 \leq r_2 \Longleftrightarrow r'_1 \leq r'_2$ for all r_1 and r_2 with non-empty $\phi_*(r_1)$.*

Proof: $r_1 \leq r_2 \Longleftrightarrow \phi_*(r_1) \subseteq \phi_*(r_2) \Longleftrightarrow r'_1 \leq r'_2$.

Thus the attribute order of a decomposition lattice for a reversible ϕ_* preserves at least an upper part of $(R, \leq)$. A similar proposition can be stated for a reversible Φ_*. Below, measures for comparing semiotic relations based on their compound representamens are defined. It can be beneficial to employ a small set of part representamens (for example an alphabet of letters) to form a large set of compound representamens (for example words and texts). This often involves ambiguous polysemy of representamens because they are used with different interpretations. For example a digit can be used in the unary, decimal, centesimal and so on position of a decimal number. Measures can therefore be defined based on the length, number of interpretations, reuse of representamens and so on of decompositions. Definition 7 only shows some examples. Many similar measures can be defined.

Definition 7. *For a semiotic relation S with a reversible ϕ, measures can be defined:*

a) $len_\phi(r) := |\phi(r)|$ *as the* length *of r.*
b) $\mu_\phi(r) := |\phi(r)_{|I}|$ *as the* number of different interpretations.
c) $rpt_\phi(r_p) := max_{(i,r)}(n \mid (i, r_p)_n \in \phi(r))$ *as the* maximal repetition of any (i, r_p).

These can be extended to measures for semiotic relations considering maximal, minimal or average values. For example, $\mu_{max}(S) := max_r(\mu_\phi(r))$, $\mu_{min}(S) := min_r(\mu_\phi(r))$ and $\mu_{avg}(S) := avg_r(\mu_\phi(r))$.

For these measures a low value is preferable. The measures should be balanced against each other. A semiotic relation that has low values for one measure need not have low values for any other measures. The signs of the decimal and Roman numeral representation of '74' are synonyms, but their measures are different: $len_\phi('74') = 2$, $len_\phi('LXXIV') = 5$, $\mu_\phi('74') = \mu_\phi('LXXIV') = 2$, $rpt_\phi('X') = 1$ and $rpt_\phi() = 0$ for all digits of a decimal number. But $len_\phi('100') = 3 > 1 = len_\phi('C')$. Therefore, in some cases, the measure for decimal numbers is better than for Roman numerals and vice versa.

So far compound representamens and signs established by their parts have been discussed, but not yet signs which have compound representamens. Because signs are triadic, a partial order for any of the three components can contribute to a partial order amongst the signs. This section suggests that an *extended denotation* of a compound sign consists of its own polysemous meanings as well as the set of meanings attributed to its parts.

Definition 8. *For a semiotic relation S with $(R, \leq)$ and a set Φ of decompositions, a sign (i, r, d) is called a* compound sign *if $\exists \phi \in \Phi$ with $\phi(r) \neq \emptyset$.*

Requiring $\sim_D$ to be an equivalence relation as in the next definition, partitions the set of denotations so that, if no homographs exist, each representamen is mapped into a partition via its interpretations. For natural language words, such conditions are too strong unless the partitions of $\sim_D$ are large and general, for example, denoting a content domain. For signs representing mathematical content, individual denotations can be very succinct so that each denotation correlates with a clearly definable concept.

Definition 9. *For a semiotic relation S with $(R, \leq)$ and a set Φ of decompositions, without homographs, for a single equivalence class of $\approx_I$ and where $\sim_D$ is an equivalence relation, a compound sign $s := (i, r, d)$ has an* extended denotation $D(s) := \{d_1 \mid (\exists \phi)(\exists(i_1, r_1) \in \phi(r)) \, i_1(r_1) = d_1, d \sim_D d_1\} \cup \{d_1 \mid (\exists(i_1, r, d_1) \in S) \, d \sim_D d_1\}$. *The extended denotation of a set $S_1 \subseteq S$ is $D(S_1) := \bigcup_{s \in S_1} D(s)$.*

Thus compound representamens lead to compound signs which are simultaneously polysemous and have potentially large sets of extended denotations. Definition 9 provides a formal explanation for why a picture might be "worth a 1000 words".

4   An Application to Euler Diagrams

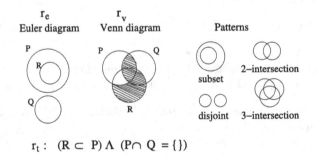

Fig. 3. Euler diagram, Venn diagram and decomposition patterns

This section applies the SCA theory described so far to an example of diagrams frequently used in teaching mathematics. The left hand side of Fig. 3 shows an example (referred to in this section as r_e) of an Euler diagram from Stapleton et al. (2017)

for the statement $(R \subset P) \wedge (P \cap Q = \emptyset)$ which is referred to as r_t. In Stapleton's terminology r_e provides a "free ride" or "observations" because it also shows that $R \cap Q = \emptyset$ contrary to r_t from which $R \cap Q = \emptyset$ can be concluded but not observed. Using SCA, r_t can be decomposed into a conjunction: $\phi_{conj}(r_t) = \{(i_{term},\text{'}R \subset P\text{'}),$ $(i_{term},\text{'}P \cap Q = \emptyset\text{'}), (i_{op},\text{'}\wedge\text{'})\}$. The representamen r_e can be decomposed into zones: $\phi_{zones}(r_e) = \{(i_{Q\overline{PR}},\text{zn}), (i_{P\overline{RQ}},\text{zn}), (i_{PR\overline{Q}},\text{zn}), (i_{\overline{PQR}},\text{zn})\}$, but other decompositions of r_e are also possible.

Figure 4 displays a decomposition lattice for ϕ_{zones} for representamens of well-formed Euler diagrams for 3 sets. Euler diagrams are considered well-formed if they do not contain triple points, adjacent lines, disconnected zones and so on (Flower et al. 2008). For many configurations of sets, it is not possible to draw a well-formed Euler diagram. Contrary to what might be intuitively expected of a partial order amongst representamens, the partial order in Fig. 4 does not consist of adding or deleting graphical elements. Instead a representamen r_1 is beneath a r_2 if r_2 can be obtained from r_1 by moving (including possibly enlarging) curves in a manner that adds zones without losing zones. Thus apart from replicating previously known partial orders, decomposition lattices can potentially provide tacit information a user was not previously aware of.

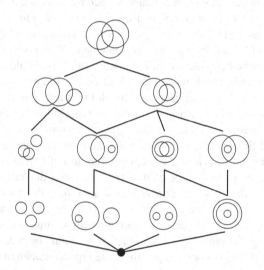

Fig. 4. A decomposition lattice for well-formed Euler diagrams for 3 sets

The patterns on the right hand side of Fig. 3 show different possibilities for two sets to relate to each other using well-formed diagrams (disjoint, intersect or subset). For n sets only the intersection of all of them is new, all other intersections affect $n - 1$ sets. Thus there are $n + 1$ patterns for n sets with respect to well-formed Euler diagrams. Considering such patterns, a decomposition of r_e is: $\phi_{pattern}(r_e) = \{(i_{RP},\text{subs}), (i_{PQ},\text{disj}), (i_{RQ},\text{disj})\}$. According to Definition 4, a decomposition has a pair for each occurrence of a part. Therefore $\{(i_{RP},\text{subs}), (i_{PQ},\text{disj})\}$ would not be a decomposition of r_e. A further decomposition that only focuses on circles might be:

$\phi_{circ}(r_e) = \{(i_P, `\circ`), (i_Q, `\circ`), (i_R, `\circ`)\}$. Each decomposition of r_e highlights another possibility for reading the diagram. Other decompositions could be defined for r_t, but compared with r_e there are fewer possibilities and the extended denotation of a sign with r_t as a representamen would be smaller than a sign with r_e as a representamen.

Table 2. Comparing semiotic relations for representing n sets

	$\|R\|$	$\|R_\phi\|$	$\mu_{max}(S)$	polysemy (for R_ϕ)	reversible
$\phi_{conj}(r_t)$	2^{2^n}	2^n	1	no	yes
$\phi_{zones}(r_e)$	2^{2^n}	1	2^n	yes	yes
$\phi_{pattern}(r_e)$	2^{2^n}	$n+1$	2^n	yes	yes
$\phi_{circ}(r_e)$	2^{2^n}	1	n	yes	no

Whether or not observations can actually be seen by users is a different question. If diagrams are too small, large or complex, users may not be able to make every possible observation. Students, teachers, experts, people with a visual disability or dyslexia will have different skills for visually parsing representamens. With respect to patterns, it is a modelling question whether patterns with more than two sets should also be considered because they are visually much more difficult to detect. In any case, Euler and Venn diagrams for more than 3 sets can become difficult to visually parse.

Table 2 summarises some measures for the decompositions of Euler diagrams. In this case all interpretations are algorithmic. Thus users only need to learn the principle of how to read Euler diagrams in order to determine all denotations. There is no repetition in the diagrams because each circle refers to a different set. The decomposition ϕ_{zones} might be positional or grammatical for Euler diagrams but is positional if it is used to shade the zones of a previously drawn Venn diagram (as r_v in Fig. 3). The decomposition ϕ_{circ} can be made positional if the interpretations include vector coordinates for the circles. The parts of r_t are not polysemous because each term has exactly one meaning. Graphical elements in r_e are polysemous because they are independent of the actual labels. For example, the same representamen (a circle) is used for every set and thus creates as many polysemous signs as there are sets. If parts are polysemous, then $|R_\phi|$ can be smaller. For ϕ_{zones} and ϕ_{circ} the polysemy is inefficiently high because $|R_\phi| = 1$.

5   An Application to Diagrams for Binary Relations

Apart from graphical representations of set theory, a further example which is also relevant for teaching introductory mathematics, is the visualisation of binary relations. The top half of Fig. 5 shows a binary relation as a set, as a matrix which contains a '1' if the row and column element are a pair of the relation and as a graph which has a node for each element and an arrow for each pair of the relation. For matrices it should be assumed that the rows and columns are sorted in a fixed sequence. The middle of Fig. 5 shows five representamens that are patterns that can be observed in a graph diagram. For a single node in a graph, the node either has no arc to itself as in r_0 or one arc to itself as in r_1. Any pair of two nodes corresponds to a representamen r_2, r_3 or r_4. The bottom half of Fig. 5 displays decompositions for the three representamens depicted in the top.

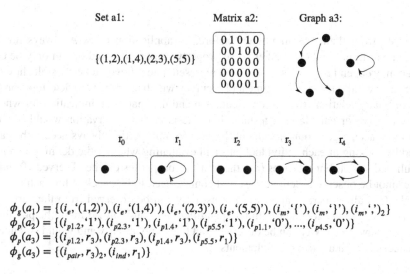

$$\phi_g(a_1) = \{(i_e, `(1,2)'), (i_e, `(1,4)'), (i_e, `(2,3)'), (i_e, `(5,5)'), (i_m, `\{'), (i_m, `\}'), (i_m, `,')_2\}$$
$$\phi_p(a_2) = \{(i_{p1.2}, `1'), (i_{p2.3}, `1'), (i_{p1.4}, `1'), (i_{p5.5}, `1'), (i_{p1.1}, `0'), ..., (i_{p4.5}, `0')\}$$
$$\phi_p(a_3) = \{(i_{p1.2}, r_3), (i_{p2.3}, r_3), (i_{p1.4}, r_3), (i_{p5.5}, r_1)\}$$
$$\phi_g(a_3) = \{(i_{pair}, r_3)_2, (i_{ind}, r_1)\}$$

Fig. 5. Different representamens with decompositions for binary relations

In the following, a_1 is used for a representamen of type "set", a_2 for type "matrix" and a_3 for type "graph". Table 3 calculates measures for semiotic relations containing only one of the three types for a set with $m = 4$ elements. Semiotic relations for a_1 and a_2 contain a maximum of 2^{16} representamens because each pair of elements either exists or does not exist. The number of different graphs for binary relations of 4 elements is 3044 and can be obtained from the sequence Number A000595 in the On-Line Encyclopedia of Integer Sequences[2]. Therefore a semiotic relation for a_3 has much fewer representamens than semiotic relations for a_1 and a_2. One could argue that the rows and columns of a matrix are also not labelled. But while it is feasible to observe whether two unlabelled graphs are isomorphic, it is difficult for larger matrices to determine whether one matrix is the result of permutation of the other one by just visually comparing the matrices. Each compound representamen of type a_3 polysemously represents different binary relations if the nodes are not labelled. The table shows that lower values for one measure usually correlate with larger values for other measures. But overall, a_3 outperforms the other types of representamens.

Table 4 compares semiotic relations of binary relations as sets, matrices or graphs with respect to whether properties of binary relations (as defined in the table) can be

---

[2] http://oeis.org/A000595.

Table 3. Comparing semiotic relations for binary relations with $m = 4$ elements

of type	$|R|$	a_i polysemous	$|R_\phi|$	$len_{Max}(S)$	$\mu_{Max}(S)$	$rpt > 0$
a_1	$2^{m^2} = 65536$	no	$m^2 + 3 = 19$	$2m^2 - 1 + 2 = 33$	2	yes (",")
a_2	$2^{m^2} = 65536$	no	2	$m^2 = 16$	$m^2 = 16$	no
a_3 with ϕ_p	3044	yes	5	$4 + 6$	$4 + 6$	no
a_3 with ϕ_g	3044	yes	5	$4 + 6$	2	yes

observed from them. As mentioned before, an application of SCA always involves judgement. In particular, whether some property can be observed or can only be computed may depend on who is observing a representamen. It would be possible, however, to experimentally measure the time and accuracy which users need to determine properties of binary relations from a representamen and use that as an indication for whether users observe or calculate. A testable hypothesis is that observation would be faster and more accurate. In our judgement, for sets (a_1) properties always need to be calculated by looking at each individual pair and evaluating whether the defining condition is fulfilled or not. For matrices (a_2) the first five properties can be observed. Transitivity cannot be observed. Semiconnex and connex need to be checked for each pair. For graphs (a_3) all properties apart from transitivity can be observed from the part representamens $r_0, ..., r_4$ together with the quantifiers 'no' and 'all'. It might be possible to describe how transitivity can be observed, but that is not as easy and would still need to be checked for many triples of elements.

Table 4. Observability of properties of binary relations

property	definition	as set (a_1)	as matrix (a_2)	as graph (a_3)
reflexive	$(\forall a \in A)\, aRa$	(compute)	filled diagonal	all r_1
irreflexive	$(\forall a \in A)\, \neg aRa$	(compute)	empty diagonal	no r_1
symmetric	$(\forall a, b \in A)\, aRb \rightarrow bRa$	(compute)	symmetric	no r_3
asymmetric	$(\forall a, b \in A)\, aRb \rightarrow \neg(bRa)$	(compute)	asymmetric	no r_1, no r_4
antisymmetric	$(\forall a, b \in A)\, aRb$ and $bRa \rightarrow a = b$	(compute)	asym. or diag.	no r_4
transitive	$(\forall a, b, c \in A)\, aRb$ and $bRc \rightarrow aRc$	(compute)	(compute)	(compute)
semiconnex	$(\forall a \neq b \in A)\, aRb$ or bRa	(compute)	(compute)	no r_2
connex	$(\forall a, b \in A)\, aRb$ or bRa	(compute)	(compute)	all r_1, no r_2

Students need to learn to switch between the different representamen types depending on a task. For example, an empty relation cannot be represented using a representamen of type a_3. A common misconception that students have[3] is that relationships between properties can be observed (instead of computed) from a_1. For example, students might think that the properties semiconnex and connex are closely connected to

---

[3] Based on personal teaching experience.

the property of symmetry because the definitions 'look similar'. In that case students are incorrectly applying an interpretation of observation to parts of logical formulas mostly because they have not yet sufficiently learned to read quantifiers and logical operators.

6 Conclusion

A purpose of SCA is to make tacit knowledge explicit. The different methods presented in this paper support this purpose. Middendorf and Pace (2004) develop an educational method of *decoding the disciplines* that helps educators to discover tacit knowledge and skills in their discipline so that they can anticipate misconceptions and difficulties that students might encounter. An analysis with SCA as presented in this paper can support such a process of decoding the disciplines by first determining what kinds of interpretations teachers use when they read and write mathematical representations and by then formally recording these as decompositions. Finally, these decompositions can be further analysed with SCA and FCA in order to detect implicit structures using some form of conceptual exploration.

The application of SCA can be quite technical as presented in the previous section. It is not intended that every teacher conducts her or his own analysis with SCA, but instead that such analyses and results are shared. A conclusion for the two examples presented in this paper is that positional interpretations are usually preferred for formal modelling and software implementations because they are easily restorable and allow a translation between different representations. For human users, however, graphical representations are often more advantageous because they have a high simultaneous polysemy which means that many statements can be observed from them simultaneously. But the patterns involved in making observations from diagrams are not necessarily self-explanatory and need to be explicitly taught. Many aspects of part-whole relationships amongst diagrams have been addressed in this paper, but many are also still open for further research.

References

Ainsworth, S.: The functions of multiple representations. Comput. Educ. **33**(2–3), 131–152 (1999)

Barwise, J., Seligman, J.: Information Flow. Cambridge University Press, The Logic of Distributed Systems (1997)

Flower, J., Fish, A., Howse, J.: Euler diagram generation. J. Vis. Lang. Comput. **19**(6), 675–694 (2008)

Ganter, B., Wille, R.: Formal Concept Analysis. Springer, Heidelberg (1999). https://doi.org/10.1007/978-3-642-59830-2

Ganter, B., Obiedkov, S.: Implications in triadic formal contexts. In: Wolff, K.E., Pfeiffer, H.D., Delugach, H.S. (eds.) ICCS-ConceptStruct 2004. LNCS (LNAI), vol. 3127, pp. 186–195. Springer, Heidelberg (2004). https://doi.org/10.1007/978-3-540-27769-9_12

Goguen, J.: An introduction to algebraic semiotics, with application to user interface design. In: Nehaniv, C.L. (ed.) CMAA 1998. LNCS (LNAI), vol. 1562, pp. 242–291. Springer, Heidelberg (1999). https://doi.org/10.1007/3-540-48834-0_15

Middendorf, J., Pace, D.: Decoding the disciplines: a model for helping students learn disciplinary ways of thinking. New Dir. Teach. Learn. **98**, 1–12 (2004)

Moody, D.: The 'physics' of notations: toward a scientific basis for constructing visual notations in software engineering. IEEE Trans. Softw. Eng. **35**(6), 756–779 (2009)

Priss, U.: The formalization of wordnet by methods of relational concept analysis. In: Fellbaum, C. (ed.), WordNet: An Electronic Lexical Database and Some of its Applications, MIT Press, Cambridge, pp. 179–196 (1998)

Priss, U., Old, L.J.: Concept neighbourhoods in lexical databases. In: Kwuida, L., Sertkaya, B. (eds.) ICFCA 2010. LNCS (LNAI), vol. 5986, pp. 283–295. Springer, Heidelberg (2010). https://doi.org/10.1007/978-3-642-11928-6_20

Priss, U.: Semiotic-conceptual analysis: a proposal. Int. J. Gener. Syst. **46**(5), 569–585 (2017)

Priss, U.: Applying semiotic-conceptual analysis to mathematical language. In: Endres, D., Alam, M., Şotropa, D. (eds.) ICCS 2019. LNCS (LNAI), vol. 11530, pp. 248–256. Springer, Cham (2019). https://doi.org/10.1007/978-3-030-23182-8_19

Priss, U.: A semiotic perspective on polysemy. Ann. Math. Artif. Intell. (2022). https://doi.org/10.1007/s10472-022-09795-1

Stapleton, G., Jamnik, M., Shimojima, A.: What makes an effective representation of information: a formal account of observational advantages. J. Logic Lang. Inf. **26**(2), 143–177 (2017)

Decision Support and Prediction

Explainable and Explorable Decision Support

Tanya Braun[1] and Marcel Gehrke[2]([⊠])

[1] Data Science Group, University of Münster, Münster, Germany
tanya.braun@uni-muenster.de
[2] Institute of Information Systems, University of Lübeck, Lübeck, Germany
gehrke@ifis.uni-luebeck.de

Abstract. An effective decision support system requires a user's trust in its results, which are based on expected utilities of different action plans. As such, a result needs to be explainable and explorable, providing alternatives and additional information in a proactive way, instead of retroactively answering follow-up questions to a single action plan as output. Therefore, this paper presents LEEDS, an algorithm that computes alternative action plans, identifies groups of interest, and answers marginal queries for those groups to provide a comprehensive overview supporting a user. LEEDS leverages the strengths of gate models, lifting, and the switched lifted junction tree algorithm for efficient *explainable* and *explorable* decision support.

Keywords: Decision support · Lifting · Multi query answering

1 Introduction

Decision support systems provide users with an action plan that is the result of considering expected utilities of various actions or learning a policy. A key challenge to decision support is building trust in the system. Often only a simple explanation is provided in the form of the action being most probable or leading to the highest utility, which may not be enough, especially if the result contradicts with a user's own assessment. Approximations may further hinder trust building, as they may be alienating to users or not good enough in applications concerning, e.g., healthcare [22]. Instead, based on exact calculations, further context, explanation, or alternatives are needed to explore the result. The problem becomes especially apparent in the health care sector. For medical professionals, understanding why they should take an action is crucial to understanding proposed actions [19]. Retroactively answering follow-up questions about groups of interest or states of patients disrupts a user's work flow. Therefore, decision support systems need to provide a full picture of alternative action plans with additional information about groups or queries registered in

---

T. Braun and M. Gehrke—Both authors contributed equally to the paper.

© The Author(s), under exclusive license to Springer Nature Switzerland AG 2022
T. Braun et al. (Eds.): ICCS 2022, LNCS 13403, pp. 99–114, 2022.
https://doi.org/10.1007/978-3-031-16663-1_8

advance. In addition to these human-centric requirements, decision support systems need to cope with vast amounts of probabilistic, relational data and still provide results in a timely manner.

Implementing such systems requires (i) a relational model compactly encoding objects, relations, and uncertainties, incorporating actions and utilities to solve a maximum expected utility (MEU) problem, asking not for a single but top-k action plans, and (ii) exact, lifted inference (using a helper structure) for accurate and timely results. Lifted inference handles groups of indistinguishable objects efficiently using representatives, which makes inference tractable regarding the number of objects [15]. Using lifted inference also enables a system to identify groups or objects of interest that act differently than the remaining objects. Using a helper structure allows for efficient answering of multiple queries, reusing calculations as much as possible.

Therefore, this paper presents Lifted Explainable and Explorable Decision Support (LEEDS). Specifically, the contributions are (i) parameterised decision gate models (PDecGMs) as the modelling formalism, incorporating parameterised utilities as well as parameterised gates for actions and (ii) LEEDS as the algorithm that outputs top-k action plans, groups of interest, and answers to marginal queries given a PDecGM, k, evidence, and possibly registered queries. LEEDS builds upon switched lifted junction tree algorithm (SLJT), which performs exact lifted inference in parameterised gate models (PGMs) [7]. PGMs represent a full joint probability distribution and consist of parameterised random variables (PRVs) that are combined by parametric factors (parfactors), which can be switched on or off using gates. We use the gates formalism [13] to efficiently model actions, explicitly encoding impacts of actions on a model by switching from one model representation to another. Modelling actions using gates also leads to fewer random variables, which has a positive effect on inference complexity. Lifting allows for exploiting relational structures during calculations [16]. SLJT performs lifted, exact inference in PGMs. A so-called first-order junction tree (FO jtree) [4,12] as an underlying helper structure enables efficient answering of multiple queries. Performance-wise, LEEDS exploits relational structures for tractable inference w.r.t. domain sizes as well as the behaviour encoded in gates, as evidenced by a small empirical case study. It proceeds adaptively to save up to 50% of its computations compared to a naive algorithm.

LEEDS as an algorithm belongs to a group of lifted algorithms aiming at performing calculations on a lifted level, using grounding only as a last resort, starting with lifted variable elimination (LVE) as the first lifted algorithm introduced [6,16,20]. The lifted junction tree algorithm (LJT) [4], first-order knowledge compilation [21], and probabilistic theorem proving [9] use a helper structure for efficient multi-query answering. Whereas the algorithms mentioned perform exact inference, approximate algorithms also exist such as lifted belief propagation [1]. LEEDS also performs lifted decision making, for which two main approaches exist: (i) finding a policy in a first-order (partially observable) Markov decision process (FO (PO)MDP) [11,18] or (ii) solving a MEU problem in a relational model that includes actions and utilities [2,8,14]. The main advantage of the first approach is its efficiency regarding decision making as it reduces to looking up the corresponding action in the policy online. The disadvantage lies in the decision coming from a black-box policy where an explanation is hard to find, alternatives cannot be easily calculated, and an exploration of the decision and a model state would be hard to achieve. In contrast, the second approach allows for explaining and exploring a decision as the model allows for further queries to provide additional information at the expense of online calculation time. To the best of our knowledge, none of the existing algorithms tackle the combined problem of decision making and query answering needed for explainable and explorable decision support, using lifting for efficiency.

In the following, we begin by recapitulating PGMs as well as SLJT for inference on PGMs. Then, we add actions and utilities to the formalism for solving MEU problems and present LEEDS. We end with a conclusion.

2   Preliminaries

This section defines PGMs [7], which combine parameterised probabilistic models (PMs) [16] and gate models [13]. Then, it recaps SLJT.

2.1   Parameterised Gate Models

PGMs combine first-order logic with probabilistic models, using logical variables (logvars) as parameters in random variables (randvars). For illustrative purposes, we use an example of an epidemic based on [17]. In the example, we model an epidemic as a randvar and persons being sick as a PRV by parameterising a randvar for sick with a logvar for persons. In the larger scheme, all persons are influenced in the same way in an epidemic without additional evidence and thus are indistinguishable.

Definition 1. *Let* $\mathbf{R}$ *be a set of randvar names,* $\mathbf{L}$ *a set of logvar names,* Φ *a set of factor names, and* $\mathbf{D}$ *a set of constants. All sets are finite. Each logvar L has a domain* $\mathcal{D}(L) \subseteq \mathbf{D}$. *A constraint is a tuple* $(\mathcal{X}, C_{\mathbf{X}})$ *of a sequence of logvars* $\mathcal{X} = (X_1, \ldots, X_n)$ *and a set* $C_{\mathcal{X}} \subseteq \times_{i=1}^{n} \mathcal{D}(X_i)$. *The symbol* $\top$ *for C marks that no restrictions apply, i.e.,* $C_{\mathcal{X}} = \times_{i=1}^{n} \mathcal{D}(X_i)$, *and may be omitted.*

A PRV $R(L_1, \ldots, L_n), n \geq 0$ *is a syntactical construct of a randvar* $R \in \mathbf{R}$ *possibly combined with logvars* $L_1, \ldots, L_n \in \mathbf{L}$. *If* $n = 0$, *the PRV is parameterless and constitutes a propositional randvar.* $A_{|C}$ *denotes a PRV A under constraint C. The term* $\mathcal{R}(A)$ *denotes the possible values (range) of A. An event* $A = a$ *denotes the occurrence of A with value* $a \in \mathcal{R}(A)$.

The term $lv(\Gamma)$ refers to the logvars in some element Γ, e.g., a PRV or parfactor. The term $gr(\Gamma_{|C})$ denotes the set of instances of Γ with all logvars in Γ grounded w.r.t. constraint C. Next, we define PGMs, which consist of parfactors. A parfactor describes a function, mapping argument values to real values (potentials). Arguments of parfactors are PRVs, compactly encoding patterns, i.e., the function is identical for all instances. A parfactor can be gated, meaning that using a selector the parfactors can be turned on or off [7].

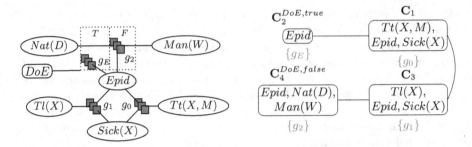

Fig. 1. Graph of M_{ex} ($Tt : Treat, Tl : Travel$)

Fig. 2. FO jtree of M_{ex}

Definition 2. *We denote a* parfactor *g by $\phi(\mathcal{A})_{|C}$ with $\mathcal{A} = (A_1, \ldots, A_n)$ a sequence of PRVs, $\phi : \times_{i=1}^n \mathcal{R}(A_i) \mapsto \mathbb{R}^+$ a function with name $\phi \in \Phi$, and C a constraint on the logvars of $\mathcal{A}$. Given a selector S and parfactors g_i (i as the iterating index), a* gate *is denoted by $\{g_i\}_i^{S, key}$, which is turned on if S has the value key and off if S has any other value. Semantically, a gate represents $(\prod_i g_i)^{\delta(s=key)}$ with $\delta(s = key)$ denoting the Dirac impulse, which is 1 if s has the value key and 0 otherwise. An assignment to a set of selectors $\mathbf{S}$ is called a* configuration *$\{S = s\}_{S \in \mathbf{S}}$, $\mathbf{s}$ for short. A PGM $M := \{g_k\}_k \cup \bigcup_{S \in \mathbf{S}} \{g_i\}_i^{S, key}$ consists of non-gated parfactors g_k and gated parfactors g_i with selectors $\mathbf{S}$. With Z as the normalisation constant, the semantics of M given $\mathbf{s}$ is given by grounding and building a full joint distribution $P_M(\mathbf{s}) = \frac{1}{Z} \prod_{s \in \mathbf{s}} (\prod_i \prod_{f \in gr(g_i)} f)^{\delta(s=key)} \prod_k \prod_{f \in gr(g_k)} f$.*

Let us specify an example PGM for the epidemic scenario, which is depicted in Fig. 1 with $M_{ex} = \{g_i\}_{i=0}^1 \cup \{g_2\}^{DoE,true} \cup \{g_E\}^{DoE,false}$. Parfactors g_0, g_1, and g_2 have eight input-output pairs, g_E has two (omitted). Constraints are $\top$ with some finite domains (omitted). In the graph, PRVs are shown as ellipses and parfactors as boxes with edges between them if the PRV occurs in the parfactor. Gates are depicted as dashed boxes, one gate for g_E and one gate for g_2, both with selector DoE. The gates are mutually exclusive, meaning when one gate is on, the other is off. E.g., the gate for g_2 allows for turning off the connection to causes of an epidemic, e.g., based on value of information.

A query for a PGM M asks for a (conditional) marginal distribution of a grounded PRV. Formally, a query is defined as follows.

Definition 3. *Given a query term Q, a configuration $\mathbf{s}$, and a set of events $\mathbf{E} = \{E_j = e_j\}_{j=1}^m$, the expression $P(Q \mid \mathbf{E}, \mathbf{s})$ denotes a* query.

Answering a query requires eliminating all instances of PRVs not occurring in the query from a PGM M. Gehrke et al. show that LVE can be used for this, which computes marginals lifted by summing out a representative as in propositional variable elimination and then factoring in isomorphic instances [7]. Given another query, LVE starts with the original model. For efficient multi-query answering, SLJT incorporates gates into the FO jtree of LJT.

2.2   Switched Lifted Junction Tree Algorithm

SLJT efficiently answers *multiple queries* in a PGM by building an FO jtree of the PGM based on selectors. In the following, we examine how SLJT leverages the FO jtree for automatically handling the effects of any given configuration.

Clusters. An FO jtree consists of clusters as nodes, which are sets of PRVs directly connected by parfactors. Each cluster is conditionally independent of all other clusters given the PRVs that are shared with neighbouring clusters. Each parfactor is assigned to a cluster that covers its arguments as a *local model*. For SLJT, clusters are based on selector values. Consider the FO jtree with four clusters for M_{ex} in Fig. 2. Cluster $\mathbf{C}_1$ is linked by g_0. Cluster $\mathbf{C}_3$ is linked by g_1. Clusters $\mathbf{C}_2$ and $\mathbf{C}_4$ are based on the selector DoE. $\mathbf{C}_2$ contains $Epid$, based on $DoE = true$, with g_E assigned. $\mathbf{C}_4$ contains $Epid$, $Nat(D)$, and $Man(W)$, based on $DoE = false$, with g_2 assigned. If $DoE(X) = true$, $\mathbf{C}_2$ is switched on. If $DoE(X) = false$, $\mathbf{C}_4$ is switched on. $\mathbf{C}_1$ and $\mathbf{C}_3$ can be thought of as always switched on.

At this point, local models hold state descriptions about their clus- ter PRVs, which are not available at other clusters. To answer queries on an FO jtree, SLJT first performs some preprocessing by making all necessary state descriptions available for each cluster using so-called messages. After message passing, each cluster has all descrip- tions available in its local model and received messages. To answer a query with a query term Q, LJT finds a cluster containing Q and answers $P(Q)$ on the local model and messages with LVE.

Query Answering. After construction, local models hold state descriptions on their cluster PRVs not available at other clusters. SLJT uses so-called messages to efficiently distribute the descriptions for correct query answering. Specifically, SLJT takes a PGM M, a configuration $\mathbf{s}$, evidence $\mathbf{E}$, and a set of queries $\mathbf{Q}$ and proceeds as follows: 1. Construct an FO jtree J. 2. Set up $\mathbf{s}$ in J. 3. Enter evidence $\mathbf{E}$ in J. 4. Pass messages in J. 5. Answer queries in $\mathbf{Q}$ using J.

To set up $\mathbf{s}$ in J, SLJT switches clusters in J on and off based on $\mathbf{s}$. Entering $\mathbf{E}$ entails that, at each cluster covering (a part of) $\mathbf{E}$, its local model absorbs $\mathbf{E}$ in a lifted way [20]. Then, SLJT passes messages. A message m from one cluster to a neighbour $\mathbf{C}$ transports state descriptions of its local model and messages from other neighbours to $\mathbf{C}$. SLJT uses LVE to calculate m, passing on the shared PRVs as a query and the local model and respective messages as a model. Messages depend on a given configuration. If a cluster is switched on, SLJT calculates a message based on a cluster's local model and messages from neighbours. If a cluster is switched off, SLJT calculates a message based only on messages from neighbours. The information from the neighbours have to be passed on to the other clusters based on the message passing scheme. For a switched off cluster, the local model of that cluster is turned off, but the incoming messages still need to be proceeded. Thus, SLJT calculates a message solely based on messages from neighbours. Given $DoE = true$ in the FO jtree in Fig. 2, the message from $\mathbf{C}_4$ to $\mathbf{C}_3$ is empty as no other neighbour exist. With $DoE = false$, the message from $\mathbf{C}_2$ to $\mathbf{C}_1$ is empty. Finally, SLJT answers the queries in $\mathbf{Q}$. To answer a query with a query term Q, SLJT finds a cluster containing Q and answers $P(Q)$ on the local model and messages with LVE.

SLJT allows for exploring a model state by answering queries. For decisions, we incorporate utilities and actions into PGMs and solve MEU problems.

3   Explainable and Explorable Decision Support

For explainable and explorable decision support, we add actions and utilities to PGMs, define the MEU problem in these models, and present LEEDS, which solves the MEU problem along with queries for groups forming along the way.

3.1   PDecGMs: Adding Actions and Utilities to PGMs

To model actions, we could introduce an action PRV with the actions in its range, enlarging parfactors. In contrast, PGMs allow for modelling context-specific independences, which can be seen as an action performed to change a model state externally. Thus, we model actions using gates, allowing for high expressiveness regarding the effect of actions on a model and keeping parfactors small, which has a positive effect on inference complexity. As for utilities, in PDecGMs, PRVs represent utilities, which are identical for groups of indistinguishable objects, leading to utility parfactors, defined as follows.

Definition 4. *Let Φ_u be a set of utility factor names. A parfactor that maps to a utility PRV U is a utility parfactor g_u, denoted by $\mu(\mathcal{A})_{|C}$ where C is a constraint on the logvars of $\mathcal{A}$ and μ is defined by $\mu : \times_{A \in \mathcal{A} \setminus \{U\}} \mathcal{R}(A) \mapsto \mathbb{R}$, with name $\mu \in \Phi_u$. The output of μ is the value of U. A PDecGM M is a PGM with an additional set M_u of utility parfactors. The term $rv(M_u)$ refers to all probability PRVs in M_u. Let $\{g_{u,i}\}_i^{S,key}$ denote the set of utility parfactors $g_{u,i}$ in a gate with selector S, switched on with value key, and $g_{u,k}$ be ungated utility parfactors. Given a configuration $\mathbf{s}$, M_u represents the combination of all utilities that are turned on, $U_M(\mathbf{s}) = \sum_{s \in \mathbf{s}} (\sum_i \sum_{f \in gr(g_{u,i})} f)^{\delta(s=key)} + \sum_k \sum_{f \in gr(g_{u,k})} f$.*

The semantics already shows how lifting can speed up performance: The calculations for each $f \in gr(g_{u,i})$ are identical, allowing for rewriting the sum over $f \in gr(g_{u,i})$ into a product of $|gr(g_{u,i})| \cdot f$.

Figure 3 shows a PDecGM based on M_{ex}. Compared to the original M_{ex}, we replace the PRV $Treat(X, M)$ with two action gates and a selector $DoT(X)$ to model treatments as actions with different effects. The two actions for the gates with the selector $DoT(X)$ are *treat patient*, T_1, and *do nothing*, T_2. Additionally, the PDecGM contains two action gates with a selector $DoB(X)$, a utility $Util$ (grey diamond), and four utility parfactors (crossed boxes). The two actions for

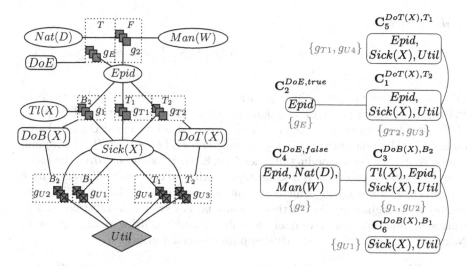

Fig. 3. Graph of the PDecGM M_{ex} **Fig. 4.** FO jtree for the PDecGM M_{ex}

the gates with the selector $DoB(X)$ are *travel ban*, B_1, and *do nothing*, B_2. As $DoB(X)$ and $DoT(X)$ select the executed action (action selector), we call the assignment of $DoB(X)$ and $DoT(X)$ an *action configuration*. Given an action configuration, either parfactors g_{U2}, g_1 or parfactor g_{U1} is on as well as either parfactors g_{U3}, g_0 or parfactors g_{U4}, g_T are on. All four actions influence the utility, albeit differently based on the condition of patients as represented by the utility parfactors. For example, sick people can infect other people. Hence, the condition of people, i.e., how likely it is that a person is sick, influences the overall utility. Sick people traveling can infect people in other areas, which increases the probability of an epidemic. Further, travelling can also worsen the condition of persons. In case many people are sick, an action is a travel ban. However, a travel ban limits people's freedom. Thus, a travel ban may also negatively influence the utility. In case a person is sick, a medical professional can treat that person. However, doctors have limited time to treat people. Additionally, treating a healthy person could also cause more harm than good. Therefore, the utility values after treating people also have to be chosen carefully.

3.2   Maximum Expected Utility

To define the MEU problem on a PDecGM, we need to define expected utilities in a PDecGM.

Definition 5. *Given a PDecGM M, a query term Q, a configuration* $\mathbf{s}$*, events* $\mathbf{E}$*, the expression $P(Q \mid \mathbf{E}, \mathbf{s})$ denotes a probability query for $P_M(\mathbf{s})$. The expression $U(Q, \mathbf{E}, \mathbf{s})$ refers to a utility for U_M. Given $\mathbf{s}$ and $\mathbf{E}$, the expected utility* *of M is defined by*

$$eu(\mathbf{E}, \mathbf{s}) = \sum_{v \in \times_{r \in rv(M)} \mathcal{R}(r)} P(v \mid \mathbf{E}, \mathbf{s}) \cdot U(v, \mathbf{E}, \mathbf{s}) \tag{1}$$

LVE already answers probability queries efficiently in PGMs, which extends to PDecGMs as utility parfactors are ignored when answering a probability query. LVE also allows for exactly computing an expected utility in a PDecGM based on Eq. (1). The inner product in Eq. (1) calculates a belief state $P(v \mid \mathbf{E}, \mathbf{s})$ and combines it with corresponding utilities $U(v, \mathbf{E}, \mathbf{s})$. By summing over the range of all PRVs of M, one obtains a scalar representing an expected utility. Equation (1) also allows for analysing which constants are associated with high utilities and computing marginal queries for these constants. For groups of indistinguishable constants, one representative query is sufficient, which lifting renders possible. Next, we show that LVE correctly computes expected utilities.

Proposition 1. *Given a configuration* **s** *and evidence* **E**, *LVE correctly computes eu(**E**, **s**) in a PDecGM M.*

Proof. Computing $eu(\mathbf{E}, \mathbf{s})$ requires LVE to eliminate all non-utility PRVs, i.e., utility PRVs basically form the query terms. Eliminating PRVs in parfactors is correctly implemented through LVE operators [20]. As utilities are PRVs, LVE correctly handles them when applying operators. After eliminating all non-utility PRVs, the remaining parfactor holds the expected utility.

The MEU problem asks for the action configuration leading to the *maximum* expected utility as in Eq. (1), defined as follows:

Definition 6. *Given a PDecGM M with fixed non-action selectors* **s** *and events* **E**, *the MEU problem is given by*

$$meu[M \mid \mathbf{E}, \mathbf{s}] = (\arg \max_{\mathbf{a}} eu(\mathbf{E}, \mathbf{s}, \mathbf{a}), \max_{\mathbf{a}} eu(\mathbf{E}, \mathbf{s}, \mathbf{a})) \tag{2}$$

Equation (2) suggests a naive algorithm for calculating an MEU, namely by iterating over all possible action configurations, solving Eq. (1) for each configuration. Since the gates in M are parameterised, the complexity of computing Eq. (2) is no longer exponential in the number of ground actions, enabling tractable inference in terms of domain sizes [15]. Instead of the domain sizes, the complexity is exponential in the number of groups forming due to evidence, which is usually very much lower than the number of constants. Assume that we observe whether a person is sick. Evidence for instances can be in the range of $Sick(X)$: boolean. Thus, X can be split into three groups, with observed values of *true*, of *false*, or no observation. For each group individualy, $DoB(X)$ can be set to either B_1 or B_2. The same holds for $DoT(X)$. Thus, in our example, we need to iterate over 4^1 to 4^3 action configurations depending on evidence.

Since LVE can compute expected utilities, one can also use LVE to solve an MEU problem in a PDecGM. For an exact solution, one constructs all possible action configurations $\mathbf{S}_a$ depending on splits due to evidence and then computes the expected utility of each action configuration. The action configuration that maximises the expected utility is selected. As the utility value is a scalar, we can easily rank them to get the top-k action configurations.

When a configuration is changed to a new one, only parts of a model are turned on or off, while the structure of the remaining model is unchanged. Therefore, while solving the MEU problem, a naive algorithm eliminates the unchanged structure twice, which is very costly. With more actions, unchanged structures are eliminated even more often. Therefore, we introduce LEEDS as a means to efficiently handle changing configurations.

3.3   LEEDS

LEEDS provides lifted explainable and explorable decision support by outputting top-k action plans and answers to marginal queries for groups of interest. Algorithm 1 shows an outline. Inputs are a PDecGM M, a number k to set the k in top-k, a configuration for non-action selectors $\mathbf{s}$, evidence $\mathbf{E}$, and queries $\mathbf{Q}$. Our example PDecGM in Fig. 3 would be M and k could be 3. There exists one non-action selector, DoE, which we could set to $false$. Evidence may be that two people x_1 and x_2 are travelling, i.e., $Travel(X') = true$ for $\mathcal{D}(X') = \{x_1, x_2\}$. Providing queries allows for registering PRVs of interest in advance, such as $Epid$ or $Sick(X)$. Then, LEEDS can answer marginal queries for propositional randvars like $Epid$ or answer representative queries for PRVs like $Sick(X)$ based on groups and constants identified by LEEDS because of evidence or high influence in expected utilities of Eq. (1).

Given these inputs, LEEDS begins by constructing an FO jtree for M based on selectors comparable to SLJT. Then, LEEDS enters $\mathbf{E}$ and sets up $\mathbf{s}$. LEEDS proceeds with solving the MEU problem, which also includes answering $\mathbf{Q}$. To solve the problem and answer queries respectively, message passing is necessary. Compared to SLJT, LEEDS has to handle utilities in its messages to pass around not only the state descriptions of its standard PRVs but also to distribute information about its utility PRV. LEEDS also has to handle changing action configurations efficiently. Therefore, we first look into how LEEDS handles utilities in FO jtrees. Then, we present how LEEDS adapts to action configurations. Last, we detail how LEEDS proceeds to compile the outputs of top-k action plans and answers to marginal queries for groups of interest.

Utilities and Messages. LEEDS builds an FO jtree based on selectors for non-action and action selectors as before. Given a configuration for both types of gates, a message from one cluster to a neighbour is calculated based on incoming messages alone or together with its local model depending on whether the cluster is switched off or on. An open question regards how to handle utilities.

Utilities are modelled as PRVs, which means they can be treated as such in an FO jtree: Clusters are sets of PRVs, including utility PRVs, possibly accompanied by a selector S and a value *key*. Local models may also contain utility parfactors. Consider the FO jtree in Fig. 4 for the example PDecGM. Compared

---

Algorithm 1 Lifted Explainable and Explorable Decision Support

---
1: **function** LEEDS(PDecGM M, number k, configuration s, evidence $\mathbf{E}$, queries $\mathbf{Q}$)
2:     Build an FO jtree J for M
3:     Enter evidence $\mathbf{E}$ into J
4:     Set up the (non-action) configuration s in J
5:     Construct a Gray sequence of action configurations $\mathcal{S}_a$
6:     $\cdot \leftarrow$ empty sequence
7:     Sorted list meu of length k with tuples $(\cdot, 0, \emptyset)$ indexed $0 \ldots k-1$
8:     **for each** $\mathbf{a} \in \mathcal{S}_a$ **do**
9:         Adapt the selectors in J to $\mathbf{a}$
10:         Adapt messages in J
11:         Calculate expected utility u
12:         **if** $u > eu(meu[k-1])$ **then**
13:             $\mathbf{V} \leftarrow$ Answer $\mathbf{Q}$ for groups in J
14:             Update meu with $(\mathbf{a}, u, \mathbf{V})$
15:     **return** meu

---

to the FO jtree of the PGM, the FO jtree of the PDecGM contains two additional clusters $\mathbf{C}_5$ and $\mathbf{C}_6$ for two gates, with $DoB(X) = true$ and $DoT(X) = true$ associated. Additionally, now $\mathbf{C}_1$ and $\mathbf{C}_3$ are also gated. The local model of $\mathbf{C}_6$ contains only a utility parfactor, while the local model of $\mathbf{C}_5$ contains both types of parfactors. Another difference is that $\mathbf{C}_1$ and $\mathbf{C}_3$ now also include utility parfactors. As $DoB(X)$ and $DoT(X)$ can be set to one action for some instances and to the other action for the remaining instances, based on splits due to evidence, the four clusters can be switched on at the same time.

Message passing follows the same idea as before: If a cluster is switched off in a given configuration, messages are calculated without its local model. The difference lies in the messages themselves, which also transport information about utilities. Thus, LEEDS calculates a probability query over shared PRVs with its neighbour (as before) and possibly a utility as given in Def. 5 over shared utility PRVs. After such a message pass, LEEDS could already answer marginal queries $P(Q \mid \mathbf{E}, s, \mathbf{a})$ or expected utility queries based on the current configurations $s, \mathbf{a}$, and evidence $\mathbf{E}$. LEEDS answers $P(Q \mid \mathbf{E}, s, \mathbf{a})$ by finding a cluster containing Q and eliminating all terms, except Q from the local model and messages, ignoring utility parfactors. For expected utilities, LEEDS answers a conjunctive query over utilities and sums out all non-utility PRVs from corresponding local models and received messages to compute Eq. 1. In our example, we only have one utility PRV, $Util$, and thus, a single term query.

Next, we show how LEEDS solves the MEU problem adaptively.

Solving the MEU Problem. Solving the MEU problem requires maxing over action configurations in a PDecGM. Again, naively, one would construct all possible action configurations $\mathbf{S}_a$, which LEEDS also has to do to obtain the top-k action configurations, over the groups elicited by evidence. The above setting of evidence in the form of $Travel(X') = true$ for $\mathcal{D}(X') = \{x_1, x_2\}$ leads to two groups of X constants in the underlying model. Given the four possible actions B_1, B_2, T_1, T_2 in gates with X as a parameter, there exist $4^2 = 16$ possible action configurations. For each configuration $\mathbf{a} \in \mathbf{S}_a$, LEEDS would set up $\mathbf{a}$ in the FO jtree, pass messages, and ask for the expected utility. At the end, LEEDS would output those $\mathbf{a}$ with their expected utilities that have the k highest expected utilities among all configurations in $\mathbf{S}_a$.

This method would compute each expected utility value for different configurations from scratch. But, we can arrange the configurations in $\mathbf{S}_a$ s.t. only one selector for one group has a changed assignment, similar to Gray codes in coding theory [10]. Let us call such a sequence a *Gray sequence*. If a configuration changes incrementally, many messages are still valid. Performing query answering with changing inputs falls under adaptive inference. For inputs that change incrementally, adaptive inference aims at performing inference more efficiently than starting from scratch. The adaptive LJT (aLJT) performs adaptive inference, handling changes in model or evidence, by adapting an FO jtree to changes in a model and performing evidence entering and message passing adaptively [5]. We use the adaptive message passing scheme of aLJT to re-calculate only those messages necessary based on the clusters that changed their status of being on or off. As selector assignments change in only one place from one configuration to the next, the changes in the FO jtree are locally restricted, which means that only messages outbound from these clusters need adapting.

In line 5 of Alg. 1, LEEDS generates a Gray sequence of action configurations. LEEDS executes the configurations in the order of the sequence in the following for-loop, adapting selectors and messages accordingly. During the first iteration, LEEDS has to set the action configuration for the first time and thus performs a full message pass as no previous setting and pass exist to adapt. In line 10, LEEDS calculates the expected utility given the current action configuration $\mathbf{a}$ and then proceeds to test whether $\mathbf{a}$ belongs to the current top-k configurations, which includes compiling further outputs for $\mathbf{a}$ if part of the top-k.

Next, we look into how LEEDS performs this compilation of outputs.

Compiling the Outputs. The outputs of LEEDS are the top-k action plans, i.e., action configurations, their expected utilities as a form of explanation, and the answers to the registered query PRV for groups or specific constants of interest. To collect the outputs, a helper variable *meu* stores the current top-k MEU solutions, their corresponding expected utilities, and answers to registered marginal queries. The queries are instantiated with representatives for groups of indistinguishable constants, occurring due to evidence. Algorithmically, the variable is a list of triples $(\mathbf{a}, u, \mathbf{V})$ of an action configuration $\mathbf{a}$, an expected utility u, and a set of answers $\mathbf{V}$. The list is sorted to easily check if a new action configuration has an expected utility in the top-k.

The body of the if-statement in line 11 in Alg. 1 concerns the compilation of outputs in *meu*. It compiles the outputs here as the FO jtree is prepared accordingly. Given the current action configuration $\mathbf{a}$ with expected utility u, LEEDS tests whether u is higher than the lowest utility at the last position of the sorted list. If so, LEEDS calculates marginals for the registered propositional randvars and marginals for specific constants as well as groups occurring in $\mathbf{a}$

or with large influence in u. To do so, LEEDS has to look at the constraints in $\mathbf{a}$ to find groups and analyse Eq. (1) for calculating u, the result could be $\{x_1, x_2\}$ and $\{x_3\}$ in our example as a result of evidence. Given the groups identified in this way and the registered queries for $Epid$ and $Sick(X)$, LEEDS answers the queries $Epid$, $Sick(x_1)$ as a representative of the group $\{x_1, x_2\}$, and $Sick(x_3)$. As the FO jtree is prepared to answer any marginal query given the current configuration and evidence, no additional pre-processing has to be performed to answer these queries and LEEDS is able to answer each query on one of the clusters (instead of the complete model). LEEDS stores the answers to the queries in a set $\mathbf{V}$. The next step regards updating meu with the new triple $(\mathbf{a}, u, \mathbf{V})$. Updating meu entails finding the position i to store the triple at, deleting the last element $meu[k-1]$, and adding $(\mathbf{a}, u, \mathbf{V})$ at i.

After iterating over all action configurations in $\mathcal{S}_a$, meu contains the top-k action configurations including their expected utility and the answers to the registered query PRV for groups or specific constants of interest depending on the corresponding configuration. At the end, LEEDS returns meu, which contains the technical output for explainable and explorable decision support. Specifically, meu is a list of length k of triples, each containing an action plan, an expected utility, and further probability distributions. Together, the triples provide a complete picture by providing k alternative action plans with high expected utility as well as information about the context in terms of probability distributions about PRVs that the user deems crucial for a decision.

Output Interpretation. LEEDS produces a list of length k of triples, each containing an action plan, an expected utility, and further probability distributions. Together, the triples provide a complete pic- ture by providing k alternative action plans with high expected utility as well as information about the context in terms of probability distri- butions about PRVs that the user deems crucial for a decision. Given an output, one can start interpreting the results.

For our running example with $k = 3$, $DoE = false$, and $Travel(X') = true$ for $\mathcal{D}(X') = \{x_1, x_2\}$, meu may contain the following items with exemplary values, with X referring to the remaining X constants and x' and x to representative instances of X' and X, respectively (per item with expected utility u: action plan, answers):

- Position 0: expected utility of 100
    - $DoB(X') = B_2$, $DoB(x_3) = B_1$, $DoT(X') = T_2$, $DoT(X) = T_1$
    - $(Epid = true \to 0.3, Epid = false \to 0.7)$,
      $(Sick(x') = true \to 0.2, Sick(x') = false \to 0.8)$,
      $(Sick(x) = true \to 0.7, Sick(x) = false \to 0.3)$
- Position 1: expected utility of 95
    - $DoB(X') = B_1$, $DoB(x_3) = B_1$, $DoT(X') = T_2$, $DoT(X) = T_1$
    - $(Epid = true \to 0.2, Epid = false \to 0.8)$,
      $(Sick(x') = true \to 0.1, Sick(x') = false \to 0.9)$,
      $(Sick(x) = true \to 0.8, Sick(x) = false \to 0.2)$
- Position 2: expected utility of 40

- $DoB(X') = B_1, DoB(x_3) = B_1, DoT(X') = T_1, DoT(X) = T_1$
- $(Epid = true \rightarrow 0.2, Epid = false \rightarrow 0.8),$
  $(Sick(x') = true \rightarrow 0.3, Sick(x') = false \rightarrow 0.7),$
  $(Sick(x) = true \rightarrow 0.8, Sick(x) = false \rightarrow 0.2)$

The first two plans do not vary greatly in their expected utility, whereas the third plan has an expected utility less than half of the expected utility of the preceding plan. Since the first two plans have similar expected utilities, one may want to compare the plans and realise that they only differ in the action for one group, namely, the travel ban for $\{x_1, x_2\}$, which only the second plan proposes (B_1). Given the results, a user could now consider additional information beyond the data encoded in the PDecGM for deciding which action plan to execute. E.g., on the one hand, a travel ban for all X may be easier to implement than a travel ban only for subgroups. On the other hand, since x_1 and x_2 are observed to be travelling, a travel ban may hit this group especially hard. Taking into consideration the results of the additional queries, the probability of $Epid = true$ is lower with the second plan, the same can be said about the probabilities of $Sick(X) = true$ for both x' and x_3. Without investing effort to finding top-k action plans and answering additional queries based on the result of an action plan, only the first action plan with an expected utility of 100 would be returned, providing few information and no alternatives.

Beyond the information compiled in meu, a user could still ask follow-up queries, from different queries for specific top-k configurations to action configurations apart from those in the top-k. The result in meu also allows for analysing which information is actually used under an action configuration. Given a travel ban, i.e., $DoB(X) = B_1$ for all groups of X, evidence on $Travel(X)$ is not used.

4 Empirical Case Study

We have implemented a prototype of LEEDS, based on the LVE[1] and the LJT[2] implementations available. Since LEEDS uses an FO jtree and LVE for its calculations, LEEDS outperforms grounded versions as well as LVE for a set of queries as shown in [3,20]. Thus, we concentrate on the following two claims: First, LEEDS performs inference faster in a PDecGM, modelling actions with gates, than LJT in a PM, modelling actions using PRVs. Second, since LEEDS ensures a minimum number of calculations to solve MEU problems and answering probability queries, by only adapting the model to changing configurations and thereby reusing as many computations as possible, LEEDS is faster than solving the MEU problem in a non-adaptive way.

We consider the running example PDecGM as input with domain sizes of W and D fixed to 50 and the domain size of X set to 10, 100, and 1000. We consider two groups in the X constants. As registered queries, we consider $Epid$ and $Sick(X)$. Since there are two groups in the X constants and four possible

---

[1] https://dtai.cs.kuleuven.be/software/gcfove.
[2] https://www.ifis.uni-luebeck.de/index.php?id=518.

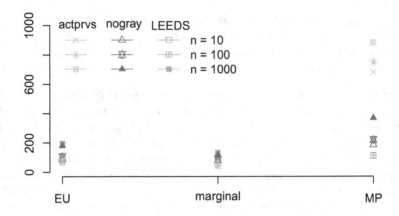

Fig. 5. Runtimes in miliseconds

actions, there are 16 action configurations to consider. Computing the same MEU grounded would require 4^{10} to 4^{1000} action configurations to consider instead of 4^2. We compare runtimes of implementations of LEEDS (leeds), of LEEDS without adaptation (nogray), and of LJT on a PM with action PRVs (actprvs). The last one requires providing the action configurations as evidence to LJT. Runtimes are collected and averaged over 10 runs on a virtual machine with 16GB working memory and no additional load on the machine.

Figure 5 shows runtimes for leeds, nogray, and actprvs. In the figure, we can see that answering expected utility queries and marginal queries roughly take the same time to answer across the different approaches. The runtimes are roughly the same as each of the approaches answers the queries on a single par-cluster, which should have roughly the same amount of PRVs leading to similar runtimes. Additionally, we can see that as to be expected for lifted algorithms, increasing domain sizes does not have an exponential influence on runtimes. The main difference between the approaches is during message passing. Nogray roughly takes about twice as long as leeds. With the Gray code, leeds roughly reuses 50% of the messages while changing action assignments leading to the speed up in comparison to nogray. In comparison to actprvs, even for this small model, leeds achieves a speed up of nearly one order of magnitude due to adaptive inference and a more compactly represented model.

5   Conclusion

We present LEEDS to provide effective decision support beyond simple explanations. To support a user in their decision, LEEDS outputs top-k action plans and answers to representative marginal queries for groups of interest. To this end, we define PDecGMs as the modelling formalism, incorporating parameterised utilities as well as parameterised gates for actions. LEEDS then takes a PDecGMs, a number k, evidence, and possibly registered queries as inputs. LEEDS solves the MEU problem in PDecGMs exactly and in a lifted way, reusing computations under varying configurations, and answers registered queries. Areas such as health care can benefit from the lifting idea for many patients and the decision support beyond explanations.

Using LEEDS as a basis, we are looking into finding attributable approximations for further speed-up. Furthermore, we are working on extending LEEDS to the temporal case to support lifted sequential decision making under uncertainty.

Acknowledgements. The research of MG was funded by the Deutsche Forschungsgemeinschaft (DFG, German Research Foundation) under Germany's Excellence Strategy - EXC 2176 'Understanding Written Artefacts: Material, Interaction and Transmission in Manuscript Cultures', project no. 390893796. The research was conducted within the scope of the Centre for the Study of Manuscript Cultures (CSMC) at Universität Hamburg.

References

1. Ahmadi, B., Kersting, K., Mladenov, M., Natarajan, S.: Exploiting symmetries for scaling loopy belief propagation and relational training. Mach. Learn. **92**(1), 91–132 (2013). https://doi.org/10.1007/s10994-013-5385-0
2. Apsel, U., Brafman, R.I.: Extended lifted inference with joint formulas. In: Proceedings of the 27th Conference on Uncertainty in Artificial Intelligence, pp. 11–18. AUAI Press (2011)
3. Braun, T.: Rescued from a sea of queries: exact inference in probabilistic relational models. Ph.D. thesis, University of Lübeck (2020)
4. Braun, T., Möller, R.: Lifted junction tree algorithm. In: Friedrich, G., Helmert, M., Wotawa, F. (eds.) KI 2016. LNCS (LNAI), vol. 9904, pp. 30–42. Springer, Cham (2016). https://doi.org/10.1007/978-3-319-46073-4_3
5. Braun, T., Möller, R.: Adaptive inference on probabilistic relational models. In: Mitrovic, T., Xue, B., Li, X. (eds.) AI 2018. LNCS (LNAI), vol. 11320, pp. 487–500. Springer, Cham (2018). https://doi.org/10.1007/978-3-030-03991-2_44
6. Braun, T., Möller, R.: Parameterised queries and lifted query answering. In: Proceedings of IJCAI 2018, pp. 4980–4986 (2018)
7. Gehrke, M., Braun, T., Möller, R.: Efficient multiple query answering in switched probabilistic relational models. In: Liu, J., Bailey, J. (eds.) AI 2019. LNCS (LNAI), vol. 11919, pp. 104–116. Springer, Cham (2019). https://doi.org/10.1007/978-3-030-35288-2_9
8. Gehrke, M., Braun, T., Möller, R., Waschkau, A., Strumann, C., Steinhäuser, J.: Lifted maximum expected utility. In: Koch, F., et al. (eds.) AIH 2018. LNCS (LNAI), vol. 11326, pp. 131–141. Springer, Cham (2019). https://doi.org/10.1007/978-3-030-12738-1_10
9. Gogate, V., Domingos, P.M.: Probabilistic theorem proving. In: UAI 2011, Proceedings of the Twenty-Seventh Conference on Uncertainty in Artificial Intelligence, Barcelona, Spain, 14–17 July 2011, pp. 256–265. AUAI Press (2011)
10. Gray, F.: Pulse code communication (1953). U.S. Patent 2,632,058
11. Joshi, S., Kersting, K., Khardon, R.: Generalized first order decision diagrams for first order Markov decision processes. In: IJCAI, pp. 1916–1921 (2009)

12. Lauritzen, S.L., Spiegelhalter, D.J.: Local computations with probabilities on graphical structures and their application to expert systems. J. R. Stat. Soc. B. Methodol. **50**(2), 157–224 (1988)
13. Minka, T., Winn, J.: Gates. In: Advances in Neural Information Processing Systems, pp. 1073–1080 (2009)
14. Nath, A., Domingos, P.: A language for relational decision theory. In: Proceedings of the International Workshop on Statistical Relational Learning (2009)
15. Niepert, M., Van den Broeck, G.: Tractability through exchangeability: a new perspective on efficient probabilistic inference. In: AAAI, pp. 2467–2475 (2014)
16. Poole, D.: First-order probabilistic inference. In: Proceedings of IJCAI, vol. 3, pp. 985–991 (2003)
17. de Salvo Braz, R., Amir, E., Roth, D.: Lifted first-order probabilistic inference. In: IJCAI 2005 Proceedings of the 19th International Joint Conference on AI (2005)
18. Sanner, S., Kersting, K.: Symbolic dynamic programming for first-order POMDPs. In: Proceedings of the Twenty-Fourth AAAI Conference on Artificial Intelligence, pp. 1140–1146. AAAI Press (2010)
19. Stalnaker, R.: Knowledge, belief and counterfactual reasoning in games. Econ. Philos. **12**(2), 133–163 (1996)
20. Taghipour, N., Fierens, D., Davis, J., Blockeel, H.: Lifted variable elimination: decoupling the operators from the constraint language. J. Artif. Intell. Res. **47**(1), 393–439 (2013)
21. Van den Broeck, G., Taghipour, N., Meert, W., Davis, J., De Raedt, L.: Lifted probabilistic inference by first-order knowledge compilation. In: IJCAI-11 Proceedings of the 22nd International Joint Conference on Artificial Intelligence, pp. 2178–2185. IJCAI Organization (2011)
22. Wemmenhove, B., Mooij, J.M., Wiegerinck, W., Leisink, M., Kappen, H.J., Neijt, J.P.: Inference in the Promedas medical expert system. In: Bellazzi, R., Abu-Hanna, A., Hunter, J. (eds.) AIME 2007. LNCS (LNAI), vol. 4594, pp. 456–460. Springer, Heidelberg (2007). https://doi.org/10.1007/978-3-540-73599-1_61

A New Approach for Employee Attrition Prediction

Lydia Douaidi[1,2(✉)] and Hamamache Kheddouci[2]

[1] École nationale Supérieure d'Informatique, Oued Smar, Algeria
`gl_douaidi@esi.dz`
[2] Université Claude Bernard Lyon 1, Lab LIRIS, UMR5205, 43 bd du 11 Novembre 1918, 69622 Villeurbanne Cedex, France
`hamamache.kheddouci@univ-lyon1.fr`

Abstract. Human resources are one of the most important assets in an organization, the success of any business or organization depends on its people achieving goals, meeting deadlines, maintaining quality and keeping customers happy. In a competitive environment, one of the biggest problems that companies face is employee departure or «Employee Attrition».

The automatic prediction of employee attrition has only recently begun to attract the attention of researchers in various industries, as it can predict employee departure and identify the factors that influence employees to change employers.

Some AI platforms are developed in order to predict employee attrition, i.e. employees likely to change employer. The objective is to help companies anticipate departures to minimize financial losses due to employee attrition. However, these prediction systems are not generic and are specific to each company. In this context, we are interested in understanding the factors that influence an employee to leave his position. We aim to develop a generic attrition prediction platform that does not depend on the application domain, based on bipartite graph properties and machine learning algorithms.

Keywords: Machine learning · Bipartite graph · Employee attrition

1 Introduction

In a context of increased competition, a competent and flexible workforce is one of the key factors on which organizations rely to improve their productivity, maintain their competitiveness and ensure their sustainability in the labour market. The issue of employee departures is taking significant prominence; retaining competent staff has become an intense challenge for organizations operating in different sectors of activity.

Indeed, regardless of the type of employee leaving, the associated organizational costs are often very high. Organizations need to review their human resource management practices in order to understand the visions and attitudes of their employees. Workplace policies that improve employee retention can help companies reduce their turnover costs.

The management of human resources plays a fundamental role in an organization's success [1]. Some studies show that the failure of many organizations originates in the poor management of these human resources, we assert that the organizations that have a reliable structure of human resources would have a means that would allow them to remain in a competitive environment. Employees have become aware of the power of their talents on organizations, they aspire to a stimulating job that allows them to use their potential and creativity to the maximum; to work in a company that would promote their learning and development outcomes.

Employee attrition means loss of employees or reduction of employees through a number of circumstances, such as retirement and resignation due to many reasons that can be professional or personal. Two terms are used interchangeably to designate the employee departure: attrition and turnover.

1.1 Attrition vs Turnover

Employee turnover: when workers leave voluntarily or involuntarily an organization and the vacant post is occupied by another employee. It describes the rate at which an organization replaces departing workers with new workers.

Employee attrition: when employee leave voluntarily and the vacant post is not filled by the organization intentionally, it is considered as an intentional reduction in workforce because the organization decide not to rehire. Employees leave on their own for multiple reasons: to take a better offer with another organization, or to make a change in their career path.

We use the employee attrition rate as a metric to measure the rate at which employees leave a company during a specified time period - typically one year - it is calculated by dividing the number of employees that left during period by the average number of employees for period, and then multiplying that figure by 100. Attrition rate helps employers to measure the rate at which the employees leave without hiring their replacements, better examine the reasons of turnover.

Turnover Classification. Internal turnover occurs when employees leave their current positions in the company and take new positions within the same company. External turnover is when employees leave their current job positions and join another company or organization. The scientific literature distinguishes between voluntary and involuntary turnover [2,3]. The authors define voluntary turnover as resulting from the employee's decision to leave his or her job, and involuntary turnover as resulting from the employer's decision to terminate the employment relationship. Thus, voluntary turnover might be functional and dysfunctional. Functional turnover occurs when a low-performing employee or employees without unique skills decide to leave their jobs, while dysfunctional turnover occurs when high-performing employee leaves and it can be avoidable or unavoidable. Figure 1 clarifies turnover classification scheme.

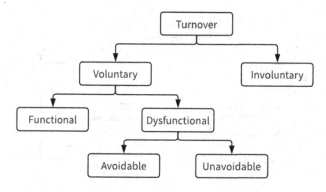

Fig. 1. Turnover classification [1]

1.2 Negative Impacts of a High Attrition Rate

In today's competitive business environment, high employee attrition is a deeper issue and can have a negative impact on a company's performance. Customers and businesses are affected and the company's internal strengths and weaknesses are highlighted. According to [4], employee attrition is considered to have a direct and indirect impact on organization's costs. When an employee decides to change a company, it might be due to many reasons including personal, organizational, and technological factors.

Nowadays, machine learning approaches play an important role in employee attrition prediction. A number of approaches have been proposed to predict turnover based on historical data such as: age, salary, daily rate, level of satisfaction, years of experience, business travel, distance from home, education field, last promotion and so on. However, there are no studies that have explored the importance of relationships between employees and their interactions.

In this paper, we aim to propose a novel approach to predict attrition based on interactions between employees using Machine Learning methods and bipartite graphs. To realize this objective, we address the following research question in this paper: Can the relationships between employees influence them to change the job?

This paper is organized as follows: The next section provides an overview of related works. In Sects. 3, the core of the paper, we present our dataset (characteristics of the dataset), bipartite graph to model employees and companies and machine learning models to predict employee attrition. In Sect. 4, we present a recapitulative table of results. Finally, we conclude and present future research plans.

2   Related Works

Many approaches were applied to predict employee attrition. Over the last decade, there has been increasing interest for relevant studies in areas including manufacturing, telecommunication industry [5], healthcare industry [6,7], etc.

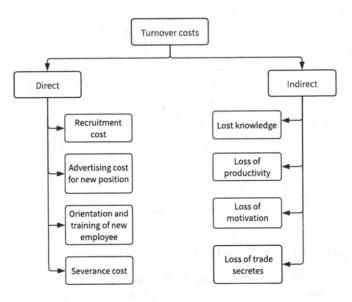

Fig. 2. Turnover costs [4]

Reference [8] aims to analyze employee attrition using logistic regression. The findings of the study, that working atmosphere, job satisfaction, and communication between manager, leader and subordinates, are the major reasons for leaving the job. Another paper [9] used Logistic Regression for the IBM HR dataset[1] when predicting employee turnover and obtained an accuracy of 85%. However, this study did not select influential features for an employee to leave the job. In [10], the authors tried several classifiers: Logistic Regression, K-Nearest Neighbor, Random Forest and Principal Component Analysis to reduce the feature space's dimensionality. They used a dataset of the U.S. Office of Personnel Management (OPM), the conclusion is that logistic regression predict attrition with the highest accuracy and the most relevant features are: length of service; lower age limit and age. The authors in [11] explored different decision tree algorithms (C4.5, C5.0, REPTree and CART). The research results found that salary and length of service were the strongest feature in the tested dataset, they recommend using C5.0 to predict employee attrition. XGBoost model and IBM HR dataset, are used in [12] in order to predict employees changing jobs. Experimental results state that the XGBoost is more accurate for predictive analysis. Other works, such as [13], also used the IBM dataset, they proposed different feature selection techniques (Information Gain, Gain Ratio, Chi-Square, Correlation-based, and Fisher Exact test) based on Machine Learning models (SVM, ANN, Gradient Boosting Tree, Bagging, Decision Trees and Random Forest). In [14], the authors developed a neural network simultaneous optimization algorithm (NNSOA) based on Genetic Algorithm which performs well for overall classifica-

---

[1] https://www.kaggle.com/pavansubhasht/ibm-hr-analytics-attrition-dataset.

tion. The authors of [15] analysed email communications using recurrent neural network (RNN) and text analysis metrics. As a result, they recommend using RNN with LSTM and GRU, which has 84,4% accuracy and 81,6% AUC. Authors in [16] proposed a novel approach to predict attrition using a dynamic bipartite graph. They represented employees and companies with a bipartite graph. Then, they employed Horary Random Walk Algorithm to generate sequence for each vertex in chronological order and apply regression to predict whether an employee intends to leave by combining embedded features with basic features. In [17], unsupervised machine learning methods (K-means clustering) are used on attrition rates to determine an appropriate segmentation and number of segments (very high, high, medium, and low). Recently, other research in [18], analyzed the dataset IBM Employee Attrition to train and evaluate several classifiers (Decision Tree, Random Forest Regressor, Logistic Regressor, Ada Boost Model, and Gradient Boosting Classifier models).

In [19], the researchers call for research that considers mental health issues such as depression, anxiety. They proposed a model to predict employee attrition rate and the employees emotional assessment in an organization with an accuracy of 86.0%.

Regarding the methodologies, some researchers are trying to predict attrition using standard methods: data on attrition are collected through methods such as interviews and surveys. Then, the analysis is conducted using linear regression, SVM, KNN, decision trees, extreme gradient boosting, etc. Other researchers proposed models that used professional trajectories to predict turnover. They generally concentrate only on the employee attrition prediction but for employers it's important to investigate the true causes of attrition [20]. The existing studies considers only demographic variables [21] (race and gender) and personal employee information such as age and salary because they are based on the same public dataset, but don't consider the importance of relations between employees to explain turnover. When an employee leaves, the culture and commitment of the remaining employees to the company can be severely affected and can cause many other employees to think about departing too. To this end, it is important to take into consideration relational variables to predict employee attrition.

3   Approach Description

3.1   Data Description

In our experiments, we collected data from a professional social network, where users can create a professional resume that contains all of the required information about education, previous job experiences, skills, training & participation, etc.

The collected dataset contains features about professional experience (job title, company name, company type, dates worked), locality of employees and other information about academic career.

3.2 Variable Extraction

In order to extract features about social interactions between employees, we present the attrition problem with a bipartite graph $G = (X, Y, E, T)$ [16]:

- $V = X \cup Y$ where X is the set of vertices representing the employees and Y is the set of vertices representing the companies, V is the set of all vertices of the graph.
- $E \in X * Y$ defines the edges between the two sets X and Y. We add an edge between employee $x_i \in X$ and company $y_j \in Y$ if the i_{th} employee worked for the j_{th} company.
- T is the timestamp of E. For each edge $e = (x, y, t) \in E$ connecting a vertex $x_i \in X$ to a vertex $y_j \in Y$, is associated a unique timestamp t representing the time when the employee joined the company.

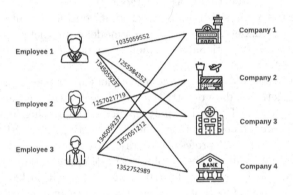

Fig. 3. A small example of how a bipartite employee-company graph can be visualized

Starting from the bipartite graph G of employees and companies, we created a monopartite projection: Graph of employees who have worked in the same companies and the number of shared companies being the weight of the link, as can be seen in Fig. 4.

In our approach, we used network centrality measurements to extract some features about interactions between employees from the bipartite graph projection.

A graph $G = (V, E)$ is composed of a set of vertices V, set of edges E. G is represented by its adjacency matrix $A = (a_{i,j})$ and N is the number of nodes in G. In our study we assume that G is weighted, undirected and connected. We briefly review some of the most important centralities:

Degree Centrality: Defined by the number of links adjacent to a node, and in our graph it represents the number of direct contacts of an employee. The degree centrality of $v_i \in V$ denoted by $DC(v_i)$, is a normalized value defined as follows [22]:

$$DC(v_i) = \frac{1}{N-1} \sum_{j=1}^{N} (a_{ij}) \tag{1}$$

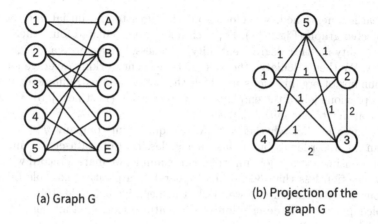

(a) Graph G

(b) Projection of the graph G

Fig. 4. (a) Employee-company bipartite graph, (b) Employees one-mode projection graph

Closeness Centrality: Measure the average shortest distance from a vertex to others. We use this metric to find employees - who finally decide to leave- who are best placed to influence other employees to change job.

In the case where the graph G is non-oriented, closeness centrality of $v_i \in V$ is defined as [22]:

$$CC(v_i) = \frac{N-1}{\sum_{j=1}^{N} d(v_i v_j)} \tag{2}$$

where $d(v_i, v_j)$ is the shortest path between node v_i and v_j.
Betweenness Centrality: represents the capacity of a node to be an intermediary between any two other nodes [23]. Betweenness centrality of a node v_i is formally defined as follows [22]:

$$BC(v_i) = \sum_{j=1}^{N} \sum_{k=1}^{N} \frac{g_{jk}(v_i)}{g_{jk}} \tag{3}$$

where $g_{jk}(v_i)$ is the number of shortest paths between node $v_j \in V$ and node $v_k \in V$ that pass through node $v_i \in V$. g_{jk} is the number of shortest paths between v_j and v_k.
Eigenvector Centrality: measures the influence of a node based on number of links it has to other nodes in the graph. This index is based on the principle that a link with a poorly connected node is worth less than a link with a highly connected node. Eigenvector centrality of a node v_i is formally defined as follows [22]:

$$EC(v_i) = \frac{1}{\lambda} \sum_{j=1}^{n} A_{ij} \, EC(v_j) \tag{4}$$

where λ is a fixed constant. n is the number of neighbours of v_i and v_j is the j_{th} neighbour of v_i.

As earlier mentioned, we added some features to the initial dataset using the projected graph (Fig. 4(b)). For each node, we calculated four different network centrality metrics: degree centrality, closeness, betweenness and eigenvector centrality. We then calculated the average time spent working (average job duration), number of organizations in which the person worked, difference in years between previous job of the employee and current job (Last new job). We added all this features to our initial dataset.

We aim to predict whether $x \in X$ will quit from company $y \in Y$ after a timespan Δt. In order to build this binary classification dataset, we annotated our dataset using average job duration. For example, we mark a record with average job duration less than 36 months (3 years) as a positive example (attrition behaviour occured), otherwise we mark it as negative example [16].

Table 1 presents the description of the features extracted and used to train ML models.

3.3   Data Exploration

The study sample included 22 167 employees. Figure 5 shows distribution of attrition in our dataset based on gender (Of the 100% employees who left, 88.9% were men and 9.6% were women and 1.5% Others).

Figure 6 shows attrition rate among 10 selected industries (we selected sectors with largest employment in our dataset), we can observe that the attrition rate in the Information Technology and Services sector was the highest among all industries (7,2%), followed by Oil and Energy sectors (3,7%). According to [24], stress because of high work pressure causes the high rate of attrition in IT sector.

3.4   Methodology

In our study we have an imbalanced dataset (a total of 75.1% of instances are labeled with class-1 and the remaining 24.9% of instances are labeled with Class-2) and most models trained on imbalanced data will have a bias towards the majority class only and in many cases, may avoid the minority class. In order to tackle highly imbalance dataset, numerous techniques have been proposed: data preprocessing methods, algorithm modification methods, cost-sensitive methods, and ensemble learning approaches [25]. We choose Synthetic Minority Oversampling Technique (SMOTE) proposed by [26] to create new instances using linear interpolation between minority class neighbouring points.

Given the dataset described in Table 1, we encode categorical data using Label encoding then we randomly select 80% of the dataset for the training set and 20% as the test set.

In this study, the extracted features were initially at different scales and some machine learning algorithms are sensitive to feature scaling (using Gradient Descent Based Algorithms certain weights may update faster than others since the feature values play a role in the weight updates). Therefore, the data were

Table 1. Description of employee features

Feature	Description
Gender	Gender of the person
Locality	City where the person lives
Experiences	Number of organizations in which the person worked
Company type	Type of current employer
Company size	Number of employees in current employer's company
Average job duration	Average duration of jobs
Last new job	Difference in years between previous job and current job
Enrolled university	Type of University course enrolled if any
Academic degree	Award conferred by a college or university
Major discipline	Academic discipline pursued by a person
Degree centrality	Score calculated using the graph
Closeness centrality	Score calculated using the graph
Betweenness centrality	Score calculated using the graph
Eigenvector centrality	Score calculated using the graph

normalized by using the z-score normalization which is calculated as follows:

$$\text{z-score} = \frac{x - \mu}{\sigma} \tag{5}$$

where μ is the mean (average) and σ is the standard deviation from the mean.

Most studies applied supervised prediction and classification algorithms capable of modeling linear and non-linear relationships between variables to develop predictive attrition models. These studies trained a machine learning algorithm using a labelled dataset that contain personal features about employees (such as age, salary) to iteratively evaluate, compare, and select variables that would predict attrition with the highest accuracy. This study investigated the ability to predict attrition using personal features and relational features to shed some light on how the individual actors influence one other to left the company. From the literature review, we selected the 8 most used Machine Learning algorithms for the prediction: Logistic Regression, Support Vector Machine with Radial Basis Function kernel (SVM), Decision Tree (DT), and Random Forest (RF), K-Nearest Neighbors (KNN), Random Forest (RF), Extra Trees (ET), Gradient Boosting (GB) and LightGBM. The classifiers were trained using Scikit-learn [27].

3.5   Results

After building the models, we evaluated them on unseen test data. Several metrics have been proposed for evaluating classification performances [28]. The four

124   L. Douaidi and H. Kheddouci

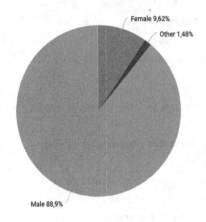
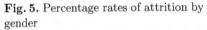

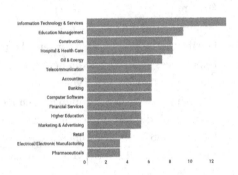

Fig. 5. Percentage rates of attrition by gender

Fig. 6. Attrition rate by industry

base performance measures in a binary classification with supervised learning approach are: True Positives (TP), False Positives (FP), False Negatives (FN), and True Negatives (TN). We present the most preferred and known evaluation metrics used to evaluate the quality of a binary classification system:

- Confusion matrix: a performance measurement for classification problems, it represents counts from predicted and actual values [24].
- Accuracy: ratio of predictions the model got right [28], defined by:

$$\text{Accuracy} = \frac{TP+TN}{TP+FN+FP+TN} \tag{6}$$

- Precision: ratio between positive samples and all the positives [28], defined by:

$$\text{Precision} = \frac{TP}{TP+FP} \tag{7}$$

- Recall: ratio of samples that are predicted to be positive and the total number of predictions [28], defined by:

$$\text{Rappel} = \frac{TP}{TP+FN} \tag{8}$$

- F1-score: Harmonic mean of the Precision and Recall [28], defined by:

$$\text{F1-score} = 2 \times \frac{Precision \times Recall}{Precision + Recall} \tag{9}$$

As we have mentioned before, to evaluate the proposed approach, we conducted experiments using a real dataset collected from a professional social network. The overall results for accuracy, precision, recall, and f1-score are listed in Table 2.

Table 2. Classification results of all the applied models.

Algorithm	Accuracy	Precision	Recall	F1-score
Logistic regression	0.68	0.59	0.67	0.63
Support vector machine	0.77	0.31	0.80	0.45
K-nearest neighbors	0.88	0.76	0.68	0.71
Decision tree	0.82	0.83	0.84	0.83
Random forest	0.92	0.80	0.89	0.84
Extra trees	0.93	0.83	0.87	0.85
Gradient boosting	0.93	0.84	0.87	0.85
LGBM	0.82	0.84	0.86	0.85

Table 2 shows that the accuracy of Random Forest (92%), Extra Trees (93%) and Gradient Boosting (93%) are significantly better, Random Forest gave the highest recall (0.89), SVM achieves an accuracy of 77% and a precision of 33%. In this research, tree-based classifiers (Decision Trees, Random Forest, Extra Trees and Gradient Boosting) worked well in general, and were found to be the top best performing classifiers. Tree based models provide a good predictive performance and easy interpretability when dealing with the attrition problem, it is straightforward to derive the importance of features on the tree decision. For this reason, we calculated features importance using Gradient Boosting model to estimate the importance of features. The results are shown in Fig. 7.

As we can see, the variables extracted from the bipartite graph (degree centrality, eigenvector centrality, closeness centrality and betweenness centrality) have a major contribution to the attrition problem, followed by the other features such as experience, company type and job duration. This results demonstrate that social connections of an employee with others can influence his decision to stay or leave the company. Managers who want to reduce employee attrition should focus on how connected their employees are with others in the organization, workers tends to leave when they are connected to another leaver or have relationships with other employees who have left.

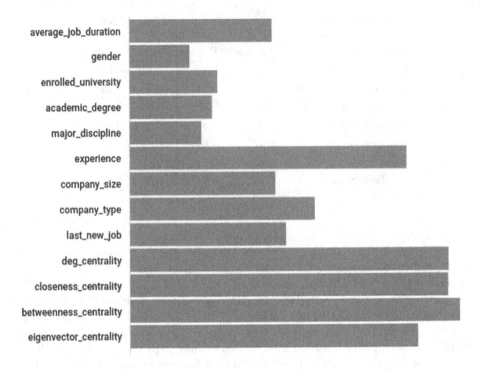

Fig. 7. Features importance using Gradient Boosting model

4   Conclusion

Companies are always looking for ways to retain their professional employees to reduce additional costs of recruiting and training. Predicting whether a particular employee will leave the company or not helps the company make preventive decisions. In this paper, we studied employee attrition problem to predict whether an employee may leave the company. We trained the models (LR, SVM, KNN, DT, RF, ET, GB and LGBM) using training data extracted from a professional social network and tested the models on testing data. Our approach integrates interaction features extracted from a bipartite graph and personal information of employees. Using the proposed approach to study attrition, employers or human resource managers have the opportunity to recognize the importance of relation networks generated by employees who chose to leave the company and by others who decided to stay. In comparison with previous works, the model demonstrated that relational features, such as the ones proposed in this research, are important and lead to a greater attrition probability. We will continue to improve the performance of our model and conduct in depth analysis by exploring the bipartite graph of employees in order to extract other type of features. Another future direction would be to examine our method in other domains such as information technology networks.

References

1. Heppell, N.: Le roulement du personnel et la performance organisationnelle: l'effet modérateur des pratiques de gestion des ressources humaines. University of Montreal (2012)
2. Dalton, D.R., Todor, W.D., Krackhardt, D.M.: Turnover overstated: the functional taxonomy. Acad. Manage. Rev. **7**(1), 117–123 (1982). https://doi.org/10.5465/amr.1982.4285499
3. Hollenbeck, J.R., Williams, C.R.: Turnover functionality versus turnover frequency: a note on work attitudes and organizational effectiveness. J. Appl. Psychol. **71**(4), 606 (1986). https://doi.org/10.1037/0021-9010.71.4.606
4. Harika, T., Bindu, N.H.: Employee retention. Int. J. Manage. Soc. Sci. **8**(03) (2020). http://ijmr.net.in
5. Suceendran, K.M., Saravanan, R., Ananthram, D., Poonkuzhali, S., Kumar, R.K., Sarukesi, K.: Applying classifier algorithms to organizational memory to build an attrition predictor model. Adv. Inf. Sci. Comput. Eng. (2015)
6. Tzeng, H.M., Hsieh, J.G., Lin, Y.L.: Predicting nurses' intention to quit with a support vector machine: a new approach to set up an early warning mechanism in human resource management. Comput. Inform. Nurs. **22**(4), 232–242 (2004)
7. Somers, M.J.: Application of two neural network paradigms to the study of voluntary employee turnover. J. Appl. Psychol. **84**(2), 177 (1999). https://doi.org/10.1037/0021-9010.84.2.177
8. Setiawan, I., Suprihanto, S., Nugraha, A.C., Hutahaean, J.: HR analytics: employee attrition analysis using logistic regression. In: IOP Conference Series: Materials Science and Engineering, vol. 830, p. 032001 (2020). https://doi.org/10.1088/1757-899x/830/3/032001
9. Ponnuru, S., Merugumala, G., Padigala, S., Vanga, R., Kantapalli, B.: Employee attrition prediction using logistic regression. Int. J. Res. Appl. Sci. Eng. Technol. **8**, 2871–2875 (2020)
10. Frye, A., Boomhower, C., Smith, M., Vitovsky, L., Fabricant, S.: Employee attrition: what makes an employee quit? SMU Data Sci. Rev. **1**(1), 9 (2018)
11. Alao, D.A.B.A., Adeyemo, A.B.: Analyzing employee attrition using decision tree algorithms. Comput. Inf. Syst. Dev. Inf. Allied Res. J. **4**(1), 17–28 (2013)
12. Jain, R., Nayyar, A.: Predicting employee attrition using XGBoost machine learning approach. In: 2018 International Conference on System Modeling and Advancement in Research Trends (SMART), pp. 113–120. IEEE (2018). https://doi.org/10.1109/SYSMART.2018.8746940
13. Subhashini, M., Gopinath, R.: Employee attrition prediction in industry using machine learning techniques. Int. J. Adv. Res. Sci. Eng. Technol. **11**, 3329–3334 (2021)
14. Sexton, R.S., Dorsey, R.E., Sikander, N.A.: Simultaneous optimization of neural network function and architecture algorithm. Decis. Support Syst. **36**(3), 283–296 (2004). https://doi.org/10.1016/S0167-9236(02)00147-1
15. de Oliveira, J.M., Zylka, M.P., Gloor, P.A., Joshi, T.: Mirror, mirror on the wall, who is leaving of them all: predictions for employee turnover with gated recurrent neural networks. In: Song, Y., Grippa, F., Gloor, P.A., Leitão, J. (eds.) Collaborative Innovation Networks. SESCID, pp. 43–59. Springer, Cham (2019). https://doi.org/10.1007/978-3-030-17238-1_2
16. Cai, X., et al.: DBGE: employee turnover prediction based on dynamic bipartite graph embedding. IEEE Access **8**, 10390–10402 (2020). https://doi.org/10.1109/ACCESS.2020.2965544

17. Zhou, N., Gifford, W.M., Yan, J., Li, H.: End-to-end solution with clustering method for attrition analysis. In: 2016 IEEE International Conference on Services Computing (SCC), pp. 363–370. IEEE (2016). https://doi.org/10.1109/SCC.2016. 54

18. Qutub, A., Al-Mehmadi, A., Al-Hssan, M., Aljohani, R., Alghamdi, H.S.: Prediction of employee attrition using machine learning and ensemble methods. Int. J. Mach. Learn. Comput. **11**, 110–114 (2021). https://doi.org/10.18178/ijmlc.2021. 11.2.1022

19. Joseph, R., Udupa, S., Jangale, S., Kotkar, K., Pawar, P.: Employee attrition using machine learning and depression analysis. In: 2021 5th International Conference on Intelligent Computing and Control Systems (ICICCS), pp. 1000–1005. IEEE (2021). https://doi.org/10.1109/ICICCS51141.2021.9432259

20. Yahia, N.B., Hlel, J., Colomo-Palacios, R.: From big data to deep data to support people analytics for employee attrition prediction. IEEE Access **9**, 60447–60458 (2021). https://doi.org/10.1109/ACCESS.2021.3074559

21. David, S., Kaushik, S., Verma, H., Sharma, S.: Attrition in it sector. Int. J. Core Eng. Manage. **2**(1), 236–246 (2015)

22. Zafarani, R., Abbasi, M.A., Liu, H.: Social Media Mining: An Introduction. Cambridge University Press, NY (2014)

23. Gloor, P.A., Colladon, A.F., Grippa, F., Giacomelli, G.: Forecasting managerial turnover through e-mail based social network analysis. Comput. Hum. Behav. **71**, 343–352 (2017). https://doi.org/10.1016/j.chb.2017.02.017

24. Forbes, A.D.: Classification-algorithm evaluation: five performance measures based onconfusion matrices. J. Clin. Monitor. Comput. **11**, 189–206 (1995). https://doi. org/10.1007/BF01617722

25. Vuttipittayamongkol, P., Elyan, E.: Improved overlap-based undersampling for imbalanced dataset classification with application to epilepsy and parkinson's disease. Int. J. Neural Syst. **30**(08), 2050043 (2020). https://doi.org/10.1142/ S0129065720500434

26. Chawla, N.V., Bowyer, K.W., Hall, L.O., Kegelmeyer, W.P.: SMOTE: synthetic minority over-sampling technique. J. Artif. Intell. Res. **16**, 321–357 (2002). https:// doi.org/10.1613/jair.953

27. Pedregosa, F., et al.: Scikit-learn: machine learning in Python. J. Mach. Learn. Res. **12**, 2825–2830 (2011)

28. Canbek, G., Sagiroglu, S., Temizel, T.T., Baykal, N.: Binary classification performance measures/metrics: a comprehensive visualized roadmap to gain new insights. In: 2017 International Conference on Computer Science and Engineering (UBMK), pp. 821–826. IEEE (2017). https://doi.org/10.1109/UBMK.2017.8093539

Author Index

Printed in the United States
by Baker & Taylor Publisher Services